Antonov Jet Twins

The An-22/-74 Family

Yefim Gordon
and Dmitriy Komissarov

MIDLAND
An imprint of
Ian Allan Publishing

Antonov's Jet Twins: The An-72/-74 Family

ISBN 1 85780 199 7

Published by Midland Publishing
4 Watling Drive, Hinckley, LE10 3EY, England
Tel: 01455 254 490 Fax: 01455 254 495
E-mail: midlandbooks@compuserve.com

Midland Publishing is an imprint of
Ian Allan Publishing Ltd

Worldwide distribution (except North America):
Midland Counties Publications
4 Watling Drive, Hinckley, LE10 3EY, England
Telephone: 01455 254 450 Fax: 01455 233 737
E-mail: midlandbooks@compuserve.com
www.midlandcountiessuperstore.com

North American trade distribution:
Specialty Press Publishers & Wholesalers Inc.
39966 Grand Avenue, North Branch, MN 55056, USA
Tel: 651 277 1400 Fax: 651 277 1203
Toll free telephone: 800 895 4585
www.specialtypress.com

Design concept and layout by
Polygon Press Ltd. (Moscow,Russia)
Line drawings by Polygon Press

This book is illustrated with photos by Yefim Gordon, Dmitriy Komissarov, Sergey Komissarov, Yuriy Kirsanov, Yuriy Kotel'nikov, Sergey Panov, Sergey Popsuyevich, Sergey Sergeyev, Vyacheslav Martyniuk, Peter Davison, Etienne Zammit, ITAR-TASS, as well as from the book *First among the First: 75 Years of the Khar'kov State Aircraft manufacturing Co.*, *Military Parade* magazine, the archives of ANTK Antonov, Yefim Gordon, Sergey and Dmitriy Komissarov.

Printed in England by Ian Allan Printing Ltd
Riverdene Business Park, Molesey Road,
Hersham, Surrey, KT12 4RG

Contents

Title page: '03 Red', a Russian Federal Border Guards An-72P, seen on final approach to Moscow-Sheremet'yevo airport in 2002. The FBG has its own small apron at Sheremet'yevo-1, and armed An-72Ps occasionally put in an appearance.
This page: An uncoded Soviet Air Force An-72 (c/n 365.720.10.952, f/n 0204) makes a low-speed pass at Moscow-Tushino in 1989 with the flaps fully deployed. The photo is autographed by Antonov OKB chief test pilot V. I. Terskikh who was in the captain's seat on this occasion.

Front cover: The An-72P prototype ('06 Yellow', c/n 006) in a very weathered finish but with Ukrainian Air Force insignia.
Rear cover, top: The An-74TK-300 prototype takes off on a demonstration flight; bottom: unregistered An-74 (c/n 47136013) at the MAKS-1995 airshow.

Introduction

Since its inception on 31st May 1946 the design bureau headed by Oleg Konstantinovich Antonov, a talented Soviet aircraft designer, specialised in transport aircraft – an area in which it soon won international acclaim. Initially known as OKB-153 (***op**ytno-**kon**st**rook**torskoye byu**ro*** – experimental design bureau) and located in Novosibirsk, it became GSOKB-473 (*Gosoo**dar**stvennoye **soyooz**noye **op**ytno-kon**st**r**ook**torskoye byu**ro*** – State Union Experimental Design Bureau) after moving to Kiev in 1953. There it thrives in the now-independent Ukraine as the Aviation Science & Production Complex named after O. K. Antonov (*Aviatsi**on**nyy na**och**no-tekh**nich**eskiy **kom**pleks **im**eni O. K. Anto**nova***; often rendered in the Western press simply as the Antonov ANTK).

The 'Union' bit in the GSOKB acronym indicated that the OKB had national importance. It is easy to see why; from the start Antonov aircraft were intended for both civil and military uses. Oleg K. Antonov's first powered aircraft, the world-famous and ubiquitous An-2 biplane first flown on 31st August 1947, was built in huge numbers and proved invaluable as a military utility aircraft and light troopship, helping to train hundreds of thousands of future paratroopers.

As the size of Antonov's transports grew, so did their military potential. The next aircraft developed by GSOKB-473, the twin-turboprop An-8 of 1956, became the Soviet Air Force's first turbine-powered transport. Over the An-10 four-turboprop airliner, this evolved into the highly successful An-12 military and commercial medium transport of 1959 which formed the backbone of the Soviet Air Force for 20 years until gradually superseded by the Il'yushin IL-76 in the 1970s.

Next, after several 'paper projects', came the awe-inspiring An-22 four-turboprop wide-body heavy transport of 1964, dubbed *An**tey*** (Antheus) after the giant in Greek mythology, which gave the Soviet Air Force true strategic airlift capability for the first time. A worthy successor to the Antey was brought out in 1982 as the An-124 *Rus**lan*** (named after a Russian epic hero). This huge four-turbofan transport was capable of lifting a 120-ton (264,550-lb) payload and this has now been increased to an even more impressive 150 tons (330,700 lb) in the latest commercial version.

Meanwhile, at the opposite end of the scale, tactical transport aircraft were not neglected either. The twin-turboprop An-24 regional airliner of 1959 served as the basis for the development of first the An-24T transport with a ventral cargo hatch in 1965 and then its improved derivative, the An-26 with a rear cargo hatch. This latter aircraft was the first Antonov transport to make use of a revolutionary new cargo ramp design – the ramp could either open conventionally for loading vehicles or slide forward under the fuselage for loading from a truck bed or paradropping. Making its maiden flight on 21st May 1969, the An-26 became a veritable workhorse for the Soviet Air Force and numerous other air arms, allowing obsolete piston-engined aircraft to be withdrawn. The aircraft evolved into a wide range of specialised versions optimised for such varied tasks as electronic intelligence, communications relay, navigation aids calibration, navigator training, ice patrol, fishery reconnaissance, casualty evacuation and fighting forest fires. Together with its progenitor, the An-24RV, Antonov's tactical turboprop twin was produced under licence in China as the Xian Y7 and Y7H respectively.

In the mid-1970s the need arose for a tactical transport offering better hot-and-high performance than the An-26. Development of such an aircraft was commissioned by India, a long-standing partner of the Soviet Union, which needed a replacement for the piston-engined Fairchild C-119 Flying Boxcar military transports operated by the Indian Air Force. In response to this requirement the Antonov OKB brought out the An-32, a derivative of the An-26 powered by 5,180-ehp AI-20D Srs 5 turboprops in redesigned nacelles instead of the forerunner's 2,820-ehp AI-24VT turboprops assisted by a 900-kgp (1,985-lbst) Tumanskiy RU19A-300 booster turbojet. First flown on 9th July 1976, the An-32 entered full-scale production in 1982 and remains in production to this day, albeit on a small scale. Most An-32s were delivered to foreign customers in Asia and South America; like the An-26, the type has seen action in

Above: The first prototype of the Boeing YC-14 (70-1873) shows off its unconventional layout utilising upper-surface blowing. Note the unswept wings, the shape of the nose and vertical tail.

The competing McDonnell Douglas YC-15 utilised a more conventional concept. Here the first prototype (70-1875) is seen as an engine testbed, with a P&W JT8D-209 turbofan supplanting the port outer JT8D-17.

a number of local wars and proved its worth more than once in humanitarian airlift and fire-fighting operations.

However, even before the An-32 came into being, the Antonov OKB decided to 'join the jet club', of which the other three Soviet transport aircraft manufacturers, the Il'yushin, Tupolev and Yakovlev bureaux (OKB-240, OKB-156 and OKB-115 respectively), were long since members by then. As early as 1967 GSOKB-473 started work on the An-60 project; this was to be a swept-wing transport powered by four 6,500-kgp (14,330-lbst) D-36 high-bypass turbofans specially developed by Vladimir A. Lotarev's OKB-478 in Zaporozhye. The project was submitted for government review in 1969 but lost out to the competing IL-76 which first flew in 1971.

Undeterred by this, the Antonov OKB began development of a new turbofan transport project in 1972. The emphasis was on field performance and the ability to operate from semi-prepared tactical airstrips close to the frontlines; the latter requirement was typical of nearly all Soviet military aircraft.

Having no prior experience with jets (aside from the stillborn An-60), the Antonov OKB had to take account of what the competitors were developing both at home and abroad. It so happened that on 24th January 1972, shortly before the launch of Antonov's STOL jet transport programme, the US Air Force issued a Request for Proposals under a programme designated AMST (Advanced Medium STOL Transport). The RfP called for quite a large aircraft intended to succeed the Lockheed C-130 Hercules; the AMST was to carry a 12,260-kg (27,000-lb) payload over a 740-km (460-mile) radius in STOL mode, operating from 600-m (2,000-ft) runways. Later the requirement was amended to include the ability to carry a 17,240-kg (38,000-lb) payload over 4,815 km (2,990 miles) in conventional take-off/landing mode.

Of the five companies that submitted bids under the AMST programme, Boeing and McDonnell Douglas won contracts on 10th November 1972 to build two prototypes each for the purpose of holding a fly-off. Both contenders were similar in general arrangement, being wide-body aircraft with a plump circular-section fuselage, shoulder-mounted unswept tapered wings with very slight anhedral and a T-tail comprising a swept fin with a double-hinged rudder and unswept tapered stabilisers; the main landing gear units retracted into narrow fairings on the centre fuselage sides. The dimensions of the cargo cabin were dictated by the need for compatibility with 90% of the US Army's divisional combat vehicles; the cabin could accommodate 150 fully equipped troops. The relatively small wings were equipped with powerful high-lift devices.

The most noticeable difference lay in the powerplant. The McDonnell Douglas YC-15 was powered by four 7,257-kgp (16,000-lbst) Pratt & Whitney JT8D-17 low-bypass turbofans in underwing nacelles carried on unconventional pylons extending straight ahead from the wing leading edge so that the jet exhaust impinged on the double-slotted flaps. In contrast, the Boeing YC-14 had two General Electric CF6-50D high-bypass turbofans rated at 23,130 kgp (51,000 lbst) each; they were installed in nacelles ahead of and above the wing leading edge to direct the exhaust flow over the double-slotted flaps. This involved the use of the so-called Coanda effect discovered by the Romanian-born engineer Henri Coanda in 1932: a high-speed stream of air (or jet exhaust) directed over the wing 'attaches' to the flaps as they are deployed, thereby enhancing lift. Using the Coanda effect held the promise of truly outstanding field performance.

The two types were developed concurrently but, since the YC-15 used many existing components (including the flightdeck section of the DC-10 wide-body airliner) to save development costs and time, McDonnell Douglas gained a head start. The first YC-15 (USAF serial 70-1875) made its maiden flight on 26th August 1975, the second prototype (70-1876) joining the programme in December. In contrast, the YC-14 was a 'clean sheet of paper' design, and funding cuts made by the US Congress with regard to the AMST programme for Fiscal Year 1974 slowed down the pace considerably. The first prototype (70-1873) was flown for the first time on 9th August 1976, the second YC-14 (70-1874) following on 21st October.

By the time the YC-14 entered flight test its competitor had completed its USAF evaluation programme, and McDonnell Douglas was able to undertake an additional series of tests with 70-1875 which had been fitted with new wings of increased span and area to meet the revised payload/range requirement. Production-standard C-15As were to be powered by 8,165-kgp (18,000-lbst) JT8D-209 turbofans with a higher bypass ratio.

Both types met their performance targets, demonstrating excellent STOL characteristics. Yet, neither was destined to see production; in 1980 the Congress killed the AMST programme altogether due to changing priorities, diverting the funds to other defence programmes. Still, these two aircraft, especially the YC-14, had a profound influence on the development of a Soviet aircraft which is the subject of this book – the An-72/An-74 family.

Above: The twin-turboprop An-26 is Antonov OKB's most widespread tactical transport. '15 Red' (c/n 9303) pictured here at Kubinka AB near Moscow is one of the Russian Air Force's many An-26s.

The An-26 evolved into the An-32 with more powerful engines optimised for 'hot and high' conditions, exemplified here by RA-48105.

Acknowledgements

Part of the information in this book comes from the reference book *More Than Half a Century of Soviet Transports* (© TAHS 2004). The authors wish to express their sincere thanks to the editorial team of ST (Peter Hillman, Stuart Jessup, Adrian Morgan, Tony Morris, Guus Ottenhof and Michael Roch) for being able to use this information.

Chapter 1

A Strange Beast

or Money to Burn

As already mentioned in the introductory section, GSOKB-473 started work on a turbofan-powered STOL transport aircraft as early as 1972. Oleg K. Antonov himself was the main motive power behind this project. He was also the one who chose to use upper surface blowing (USB) for the future aircraft, describing it to his design staff as 'a mighty jet of gases passing over the wings at great speed to generate additional lift'. So strong was Antonov's faith in the Coanda effect as a means of achieving the required field performance that other, more conventional powerplant arrangements were hardly considered at all.

The new transport received the tentative in-house designation 'aircraft 200'. By comparison, the An-22 had been called 'aircraft 100' at the design phase, while the future An-124 'big lifter' then under development was known at the Antonov OKB as 'aircraft 400'. Designer Ya. G. Orlov was appointed the aircraft's project chief.

At first the work proceeded as a private venture because, believe it or not, the OKB had a certain amount of money left over *which it had two spend on something*! (Something worthwhile, that is.) Fact is, a quirk of the Soviet system of state funding was that if the amount allocated to a given enterprise from the state budget was not used completely, the enterprise was not allowed to 'keep the change' and use it as it saw fit. The amount 'saved' was withdrawn and, worst of all, the funding for the following year was cut back accordingly. Being thrifty simply did not pay!

Later, however, the 'aircraft 200' proposal won support from the Soviet Air Force General Headquarters which encouraged the development of a light tactical transport suitable for airlifting personnel and materiel to tactical airstrips near the forward edge of the battle area, as well as delivering supplies to auxiliary airfields occupied by combat aircraft. A joint team representing GSOKB-473, the Air Force's Department of Procurement and the Ministry of Aircraft Industry (MAP – *Mini**ster**stvo aviatsi**on**noy pro**mysh**lennosti*) drew up the specific operational requirement (SOR) for the aircraft. The Antonov OKB's proposal envisaged an aircraft comparable in size and payload to the An-26 (the maximum payload was originally 5 tons/11,020 lb), with STOL capability and paradropping capability. Its tactical *mode d'emploi* presupposed fairly small dimensions (to facilitate operations into small airstrips surrounded by obstacles and allow the aircraft to be hidden under camouflage netting), a high rate of climb and, not least, a sturdy airframe able to withstand the augmented loads on semi-prepared runways.

In due course the preliminary design project passed all the required reviews, and 'aircraft 200' gained official status. On 26th June 1973 the Soviet Union's Communist party Central Committee and the Soviet Council of Ministers issued joint directive No.533-186 ordering development of a light STOL transport aircraft which received the official designation An-72. A joint decision to the same effect by MAP, the Ministry of Civil Aviation (MGA – *Mini**ster**stvo grazh**dahn**skoy avi**ah**tsii*) and the Soviet Air Force followed on 27th May 1974. The SOR for the new aircraft was mutually approved by MAP, MGA and the Soviet State Aircraft Register in April-May 1975. State funding could now be secured for the An-72 programme.

Development of the 'aircraft 200' proceeded at an incredible pace. The aircraft shared the general arrangement of the Boeing YC-14, featuring shoulder-mounted wings with very little sweep, a T-tail and two turbofan engines mounted as close to the fuselage as possible ahead of the wing leading edge to exhaust over the upper surface and inboard flaps. Probably wishing to forestall possible accusations of 'copying', Oleg K. Antonov wrote in a memo, *'We selected this arrangement not because we wanted to emulate the Boeing YC-14, which is a very interesting design, but in order to protect the engines from foreign-object damage, which might be a problem in the harsh conditions of the Siberian winter. Good short-field performance and FOD prevention measures are 'musts' for an aircraft that will operate from semi-prepared runways – sometimes runways of chance.'*

Whatever Antonov may have said or written, he and his design team were clearly inspired by the YC-14; apart from the general arrangement, the future An-72 shared some specific design features of the American transport. In fact, an early desktop model of the An-72 bearing the symbolic registration CCCP-1975 (possibly a hint at the first flight date envisaged originally) showed a staggering similarity to the YC-14 – even the shape of the flightdeck section, the vertical tail and the main landing gear fairings were identical.

However, looking for inspiration is one thing but direct copying is another – and the An-72 was by no means a straight copy of the Boeing design. Firstly, the An-72 was rather smaller, as will be evident from the table on page 8. Secondly, the outlines of the aircraft changed perceptibly in the course of the design work, and the final design that was frozen in 1976 looked rather different from the YC-14, incorporating both Antonov OKB tradition and the work of hundreds of engineers, much of which had to be done from scratch.

The future of the project depended heavily on the availability of a suitable powerplant, and a suitable engine existed; it was the aforementioned Lotarev D-36 turbofan rated at

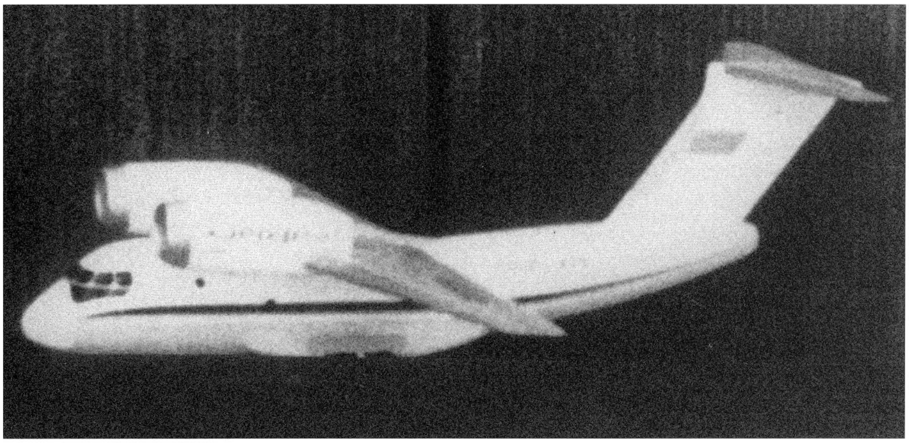

An early desktop model of the An-72. The similarity to the YC-14 is obvious.

Above: Another aspect of the same model from an Aviaexport brochure; note the shape of the vertical tail, the nose and the main gear fairings.

Centre and above: This model from the Antonov ANTK museum represents the real thing – except that the original version of the An-72 never flew in Soviet Air Force colours. Note the rear strakes.

6,500 kgp (14,330 lbst). Originally developed for the stillborn An-60, it had a happier fate than the aircraft it was to power; the D-36 found use on the Yakovlev Yak-42 trijet short/medium-haul airliner which first flew in 1974. Oleg K. Antonov was known as a staunch proponent of fuel-efficient turboprop engines; yet, only a high-bypass turbofan with a high mass flow, such as the D-36, made it possible to use the Coanda effect on which the An-72's concept was based.

Other points in favour of the D-36 included its low specific fuel consumption (SFC) which was on a par with the best Western turbofans. Importantly, the engine had a relatively low exhaust gas temperature, which was crucial for an aircraft embodying the USB concept; duralumin alloys, which were (and still are) the principal structural material in contemporary aviation, start melting at temperatures as low as 150°C (302°F), and measures had to be taken to avoid compromising the aircraft's structural integrity. A further bonus was the D-36's modular design facilitating repairs and long service life. Finally, the engine had entered quantity production at aero engine plant No.478 in Zaporozhye, its birthplace, and reached an adequate operational reliability level.

Wind tunnel tests confirmed the calculations made by the Antonov OKB's engineers. The lift increase generated by the Coanda effect was sizeable, reaching 20% in certain flight modes when the flaps were deployed; the exhaust jets adhering to the flaps improved the lift/drag ratio considerably on take-off and landing approach. Since the wings, engines and flaps all contributed to generating lift, a large amount of research had to be done on ground rigs to explore the interaction of these components. In order to maximise the lift increase generated by USB the engine nozzles were given a flattened shape to spread the exhaust flow over the flaps.

The wings, which in their ultimate configuration had an area of 89.6 m^2 (963.4 sq ft), were equipped with three-section full-span leading-edge slats (in contrast, the YC-14, like many other Boeing jets, had Krueger flaps). The trailing edge was occupied by double-slotted flaps on the large-span centre section carrying the engines and triple-slotted flaps on the detachable outer wings inboard of the one-piece ailerons. There were two spoiler sections on each side of the wing centre section ahead of the inboard flaps, plus four on each outer wing ahead of the outboard flaps. The centre section spoilers were actually airbrakes deploying automatically on touchdown or in the event of an aborted take-off. The outer wing spoilers were used for roll control in cruise flight and as lift dumpers, increasing the glideslope angle during approach to short airstrips.

The ground spoilers (airbrakes) enhanced overall braking efficiency by 20%. Additionally, the engines were provided with bucket-type thrust reversers (of the same design as on the YC-14), and a brake parachute was housed in the fuselage tailcone as a last resort. It was enclosed by vertically split doors reminiscent of the airbrake petals on the Fokker F.28 Fellowship and the later British Aerospace 146.

Besides the obvious advantages it conferred, the USB concept had some drawbacks as well. Wind tunnel research revealed that the exhaust jets passing over the wings generated vortices aft of the wings, especially at the wing/fuselage joint. The distribution of these vortices, which depended on the angle of attack (AOA), speed and engine rpm, could affect the aircraft's stability considerably. To minimise these harmful effects the Antonov OKB engineers augmented the An-72's tail unit with two large outward-canted strakes of trapezoidal planform flanking the cargo hatch in the manner of the An-26 and An-32 to reduce airflow interference; the YC-14 had no such strakes. To increase the operational AOA range and provide longitudinal trimming the An-72 had variable-incidence tailplanes. These utilised a special inverted airfoil with a flat upper surface and featured so-called deflectors (inverted leading-edge slats deploying simultaneously with flap extension) to eliminate the possibility of deep stall – a problem affecting aircraft with T-tails.

The vertical tail was quite large for the size of the aircraft and, in common with the YC-14, featured an unusual double-hinged rudder. Unlike the American jet, whose rudder was split into three sections along the entire chord, the An-72 had a 'solid' forward rudder segment, only the trailing-edge segment being split into upper and lower halves. Of these, the lower half was controlled directly by the rudder pedals; the others were controlled by hydraulic actuators, the forward segment deflecting automatically to compensate for the thrust asymmetry caused by an engine failure.

The rudder, ailerons and elevators were mass-balanced and aerodynamically balanced to reduce the control forces within a wide range of flight speeds and CG positions; the lower rear rudder segment featured a trim tab, while the ailerons and elevators incorporated both trim tabs and servo tabs. This allowed the pilots to balance the aircraft as the flaps were deployed – a process that changed the An-72's aerodynamics dramatically (at low speed the aircraft would be, as one source put it, literally 'suspended' on the engine thrust due to the Coanda effect) – and fly the aircraft in manual mode if the hydraulic control actuators failed.

The freight hold, which in the final project configuration was 9 m (29 ft 6$\frac{21}{64}$ in) long, 2.2 m (7 ft 2$\frac{5}{8}$ in) wide and 2.1 m (6 ft 10$\frac{43}{64}$ in) high, could accommodate a wide range of military loads. These included up to 32 fully equipped troops, a GAZ-66 four-wheel-drive army lorry (the Soviet counterpart of the Bedford RL/RLW and Bedford MJ), two GAZ-69 or UAZ-469 jeeps, aircraft engines, as well as standard air freight containers (the smaller varieties) or pallets. Like its turboprop-pow-

The fuselage of the An-72's full-scale mock-up at the Antonov OKB's experimental plant at Kiev-Svyatoshino.

	An-72 project	YC-14
Powerplant	2 x Lotarev D-36	2 x General Electric CF6-50D
Engine thrust, kgp (lbst)	2 x 6,450 (2 x 14,220) *	2 x 23,130 (2 x 51,000)
Wing span	26.2 m (85 ft 11½ in) *	39.32 m (129 ft 0 in)
Wing area, m^2 (sq ft)	86.78 (933.11) *	163.7 (1,762)
Wing sweep at quarter-chord	14°	n.a.
Wing aspect ratio	7.65	n.a.
Length overall	25.91 m (85 ft 0 in) *	40.13 m (131 ft 8 in)
Height on ground	8.25 m (27 ft $0\frac{13}{16}$ in) *	14.73 m (48 ft 4 in)
Max. fuselage diameter	3.1 m (10 ft $2\frac{3}{64}$ in)	5.44 m (17 ft 10 in)
Tailplane span	n.a. †	16.68 m (54 ft 8½ in)
Landing gear track	4.15 m (13 ft $7\frac{25}{64}$ in)	5.66 m (18 ft 7 in)
Landing gear wheelbase (static)	7.08 m (23 ft 2¾ in)	12.50 m (41 ft 0 in)
Freight hold dimensions:		
length, less ramp	9.0 m (29 ft $6\frac{21}{64}$ in)	14.43 m (47 ft 4 in)
width	2.4 m (7 ft 2⅝ in)	3.50-3.55 m (11 ft 6 in to 11 ft 8 in)
height	2.2 m (7 ft 2⅝ in)	3.40-3.66 m (11 ft 2 in to 12 ft 0 in)
MTOW, kg (lb)	28,500 (62,830) *	
Max. payload, kg (lb)	5,000 (11,020)	77,110 (170,000) / 107,500 (237,000) ‡
Max. fuel load, kg (lb)	8,900 (19,620)	30,120 (66,400)
Cruising speed, km/h (mph)	720 (447) §	723 (449)
Range with reserves, km (miles):		
with a 4.5-ton (9,920-lb) payload	800 (496)	740 (460) ¶
with max fuel	2,550 (1,583)	n.a.
Ferry range, km (miles)	n.a.‖	5,133 (3,190)

* Data different from those of the actual prototype
† 10.0 m (32 ft $9\frac{45}{64}$ in) on the actual aircraft
‡ STOL/normal mode
§ At 8,000 m (26,250 ft)
¶ Operating radius (payload unknown)
‖ 3,200 km (1,987 miles) on the actual prototype

ered An-26 and An-32 stablemates, the An-72 featured a cargo ramp of patented Antonov design. This could be either lowered conventionally for loading/unloading vehicles and embarking/disembarking troops or slid forward under the fuselage for straight-in loading from a truck bed or paradropping. Unlike the An-26/An-32, however, the ramp did not close the aperture completely; two clamshell cargo doors and a hinged rear pressure bulkhead were installed aft of it.

Special attention was given to designing the An-72's landing gear. The ability to operate from tactical dirt or snow airstrips was a standing requirement for almost all Soviet military aircraft. All previous Antonov aircraft were capable of soft-field operations, and the An-72 should be no exception to the rule. Now, however, the ability to operate from soggy or uneven runways was also specified.

The OKB contemplated close to 30 versions of landing gear design, including an air cushion landing gear. To verify the latter option an An-14 Pcholka (Honeybee) piston-engined utility aircraft was modified to become the An-714 – a landing gear testbed with three independent air cushion units supplanting the standard wheels. The results proved disappointing; the rough-runway capability afforded by the air cushion landing gear did not justify the complication of the aircraft's design, complicated operational procedures, weight penalty and extra drag. Also, the rubberised skirt containing the air cushion was not durable enough and the whole idea was deemed impractical.

CCCP-19774 (c/n 004), the first prototype An-72, wore a non-standard Aeroflot livery with the titles/logo on the engine nacelles, 'An-72' nose titles in red on white (instead of in white on the blue cheatline) and a dark grey common main gear fairing. A ground power cable is hooked up to the aircraft.

Top: CCCP-19774 parked on the grass in a remote corner of Kiev-Svyatoshino. Note the nose-mounted landing/taxi lights and the aerial above the flightdeck.
Above: The aircraft makes a high-speed run with the high-lift devices fully deployed. Note the cine cameras on the wings and fin.

Above: An-72 CCCP-19774 takes off from Kiev-Svyatoshino with KiAPO's pre-delivery line featuring Aeroflot An-24s and Soviet Air Force An-26s and one of the assembly buildings in the background.

The first prototype takes off from a grass field partly covered by snow during rough-field tests.

Above: The first prototype climbs away, showing the flaps at 10° take-off setting, the shape of the engine nozzles, the brake parachute doors forming the rear extremity of the fuselage, the splayed ventral strakes and the position of the communications radio's upper blade aerial on top of the starboard engine nacelle.

Still in take-off configuration, CCCP-19774 flies at high altitude, No APU appears to be installed yet in the starboard rear portion of the main gear fairing. Note also the thin, flat-topped rear portion of the fin/tailplane fairing.

Above and below: Shortly after the beginning of the flight tests CCCP-19774 was fitted with a modified radome incorporating a long pointed air data probe. Note the heat shields and soot deposits on the wings' upper surface aft of the engine nozzles; the D-36 is not famous for being an Old Smokie, but still...

Above and below: Two more aspects of the first prototype flying in the vicinity of Kiev during manufacturer's flight tests. The low wing aspect ratio and the close proximity of the engines to the fuselage are evident. Note also the lack of trailing-edge sweep on the wings and tailplanes.

Above: A 1968-model GAZ-24 Volga sedan is driven up the ramp, using the detachable vehicle loading ramps. Note that the tips of the flap track fairings are painted red for conspicuity to prevent damage by ground vehicles. The entry door opens through 90° and can be opened hydraulically in flight for bailing out.

For low-speed/high-alpha tests the first prototype, by then reregistered CCCP-83966 and lacking the ventral strakes, was fitted with a spin recovery parachute. Note the missing probe aerial at the top of the fin and the cine camera 'egg' under the port stabiliser at about half-span.

The arrangement selected eventually was an ordinary retractable undercarriage with a twin-wheel nose unit and two independent main units in tandem on each side, all with levered suspension – just like on the YC-14. Unlike the latter, however, the nose unit retracted forwards; the main units had a single wheel each instead of two and retracted inwards, not upwards and aft. The An-72's main gear fairings were, in effect, blended into a common fairing wrapped around the fuselage underside. The energy absorption characteristics of the hefty oleo struts were designed to allow the aircraft to negotiate a so-called 'standard hump' (a term used for describing the runway's condition and hence the possibility of operating a given aircraft from it) up to 35 cm (13¾ in) high. To enhance flight safety the designers dispensed with the main gear uplocks which could be fouled by mud or snow/slush on unprepared airstrips and then jam; the main gear units rested on the closed mainwheel well doors when retracted, extending under their own weight when the doors opened. In the event of a hydraulic system failure the landing gear was locked down mechanically; if one main gear strut refused to extend, the aircraft could land safely on the other three.

Bigger-than-average strength reserves were incorporated into the An-72's airframe with possible hard landings and bumpy runways in mind, which led to excess structural weight. To offset this weight penalty the OKB made large-scale use of advanced structural materials and manufacturing technologies: high-strength aluminium alloys, titanium fasteners, honeycomb structures and bonding, and composites (glassfibre reinforced plastic

Above and below: All set to go to Paris. A few days before Le Bourget '79, with the exhibit code 350 already applied, the first prototype shows off its new colour scheme (in full conformity with the current standard) and the restyled rear end at a display for Soviet government officials.

Flaps almost retracted, the An-72 taxies in at Paris-Le Bourget after touching down on foreign soil for the first time. Note the teardrop fairings enclosing the rear hinges of the clamshell cargo doors whose joint line is visible. The cheatline terminates at the manufacturing joint between the rear fuselage section and the large tailcone. Note the cranked fin trailing edge.

and carbonfibre reinforced plastic). The total weight of GRP and CFRP components amounted to 875 kg (1,930 lb), which gave an overall weight saving of 350 kg (771 lb).

The table on page 8 gives a comparison of the An-72 and the YC-14. The An-72 figures are project data coming from an early Aviaexport ad, but there are reasons to believe that it was the penultimate project version, as some of the dimensions differ from what is normally quoted for the prototype.

As the detail drawings and other manufacturing documents were issued and transferred to the OKB's experimental production facility at Kiev-Svyatoshino airfield, prototype construction gradually got under way. Engineer A. Romanyuk was put in charge of the manufacturer's flight tests and preparations for same.

The Kiev-built prototype batch comprised six aircraft; the static test article (construction number 001 – that is, Batch 0, 01st aircraft in the batch) came first, followed by the first fatigue test airframe (c/n 002) and what was originally the second fatigue test airframe (c/n 003). By the early summer of 1977 the OKB's experimental plant had completed the first flying prototype (c/n 004) which received the meaningful registration CCCP-19774 – that is, year of production 1977, 4th airframe built.

On 31st August 1977, having passed the required ground checks and taxi tests, the An-72 successfully made its maiden flight, making the customary short hop from Svyatoshino to the OKB's flight test facility at Kiev-Gostomel' north-west of the city. The date was hardly a matter of chance: the first flight of the first Antonov jet took place exactly 30 years after the OKB's firstling, the An-2, had taken to the air in Novosibirsk.

On its maiden flight CCCP-19774 was flown by the Antonov OKB's chief test pilot V. I. Terskikh, with A. L. Kroots as flight engineer. Both crew members were unanimous in their appraisal of the aircraft, describing it as 'a pleasure to fly'. The An-72 was easy to fly and responsive to the controls; the good flightdeck ergonomics, state-of-the-art instrumentation and avionics, and low noise levels also earned high praise.

What mattered the most, however, was the An-72's excellent flight performance. The STOL performance target had been met: with a normal take-off weight and up to 3,500 kg (7,720 lb) of payload the aircraft became airborne at 185 km/h (115 mph) within 420-450 m (1,380-1,480 ft). The An-72's rate of climb was described as 'leaping into the sky'. During landing approach the aircraft descended steeply enough to put unaware onlookers into an 'oh-no-it's-going-to-crash' state of mind, remaining controllable at airspeeds right down to 165 km/h (102 mph). During demonstration flights the An-72 operated into dirt strips just 1,000 m (3,280 ft) long, coming to a halt after no more than 350 m (1,150 ft), and performed single-engine take-offs. The normal payload was 5,000 kg (11,020 lb), but in high gross weight configuration the aircraft could carry up to 7,500 kg (16,530 lb) of cargo.

Of course, an aircraft with such unconventional looks was bound to earn nicknames. Some airmen looked at the aircraft's air intakes raised above the fuselage in a head-on view and bestowed the nickname *Cheburashka* on the An-72. (Cheburashka is a popular Soviet cartoon character created by writer Eduard Uspenskiy back in the early 1970s, a nondescript but cute furry little creature with huge circular ears looking like a Teenage Mutant Mickey Mouse.) Others took in the hunchbacked profile and dubbed the machine *Verblyud* (Camel).

To speed up the tests the second fatigue test airframe was converted to flight test status in 1979, receiving the custom registration CCCP-19793 (that is, 1979, airframe No.3). In the same fashion the third prototype (c/n 005) was registered CCCP-19795.

Above: The second prototype, CCCP-19793 (c/n 003), as originally flown with splayed ventral strakes and, apparently, a brake parachute. Note that the dorsal blade aerial has been moved from the starboard engine nacelle, where it was vulnerable to jet blast in reverse thrust mode, to the top of the fin.

The same aircraft following modifications to the same standard as CCCP-83966; note the extra flush antenna built into the fin below the Soviet flag. The paintwork in the starboard engine's inlet duct appears to be chipped. The landing/taxi lights are still located immediately aft of the radome.

Above: Another view of CCCP-19793 in updated form, showing the increased-area lower rear rudder segment and restyled tailcone. On the ground the elevators were always locked at maximum downward deflection to ease the load on the hydraulic actuator.

As originally flown the second prototype was outwardly identical to the first prototype, except that it had full 1973-standard Aeroflot colours (the first aircraft had a non-standard livery). Soon, however, a number of changes were introduced. Firstly, the brake parachute proved of little use at the An-72's low landing speeds; therefore it was deleted and the vertically split clamshell doors gave way to a longer 'solid' tailcone flattened from below, in the manner of the YC-14. The strakes on the aft fuselage sides proved unnecessary and were eliminated as well, exposing the small teardrop fairings which enclosed the rear hinges of the clamshell cargo doors. The first two prototypes were modified in this fashion.

Another alteration concerned the doors proper. Firstly, they created harmful vortices when opened in flight, complicating flying; secondly, on the ground they could become an obstacle, preventing vehicles from backing all the way up to the freight hold floor for loading and unloading. Hence CCCP-19795 introduced a new cargo door design with a one-piece door aft of the ramp; this door dropped down an inch or so before sliding aft on a centreline track to lie flat against the underside of the tailcone. The door, which was made of CFRP, was the largest single composite structure in the An-72's airframe.

The third prototype, CCCP-19795 (c/n 005) was displayed at the 1981 Paris Air Show with the exhibit code 352.

Top and above: Seen here at Kiev-Svyatoshino, CCCP-19795 introduced a one-piece sliding rear cargo door. Note also the APU exhaust below the emergency exit and the landing/taxi lights relocated to the front portions of the main gear fairing.

Above: An-72 CCCP-19795 is apparently seen here at Khar'kov-Sokol'nikovo, the airfield of aircraft factory No 135, in company with a Tu-134UBL military crew trainer and a Tu-134 *Balkany* airborne command post.

To improve directional stability and control, concurrently with the deletion of the ventral strakes the area of the rudder's lower rear segment was increased by increasing its root chord. The result was a kinked trailing edge of the vertical tail characteristic of all An-72s since 1979. To reduce interference drag the rear portion of the fin/tailplane fairing was given a characteristically bulged shape. The dorsal blade aerial serving the communications radio was relocated from its original position atop the starboard engine nacelle on CCCP-19774, where it could be damaged by jet blast when reverse thrust was applied, to the top of the fin. Concurrently a second flush antenna for an air traffic control (ATC) transponder was added on each side of the fin below the existing short-range radio navigation system (SHORAN) antenna. On CCCP-19795 the landing/taxi lights were relocated from the fuselage nose to the main landing gear fairing.

Certain problems associated with the Coanda effect surfaced in the course of the manufacturer's flight tests. The aerodynamics of the actual aircraft were somewhat different from the results obtained in wind tunnels; the adherence of the jet efflux to the wings was variable, depending on the flight mode (climb, cruise and so on) and other factors, notably wind direction (a tailwind would disrupt the smooth flow). The rear portions of the engine nacelles and the thrust reverser doors were altered several times in an attempt to stabilise the flow. An engine failure created a difference in lift so strong that the aircraft would immediately try to roll over on its back, requiring prompt corrective action. The problem was cured by introducing a feature which automatically deployed the roll control spoiler on the opposite wing (that is, the live-engine side) to counter the roll.

Nevertheless, the general appraisal of the An-72's fundamental concept was positive. As was often the case in the Soviet Union, a

An-72 CCCP-19795 at the 34th Paris Air Show in 1981, with a mobile gangway parked alongside to facilitate boarding for invited guests. This view shows the An-72's characteristic collapsible air intake covers which fold to save storage space

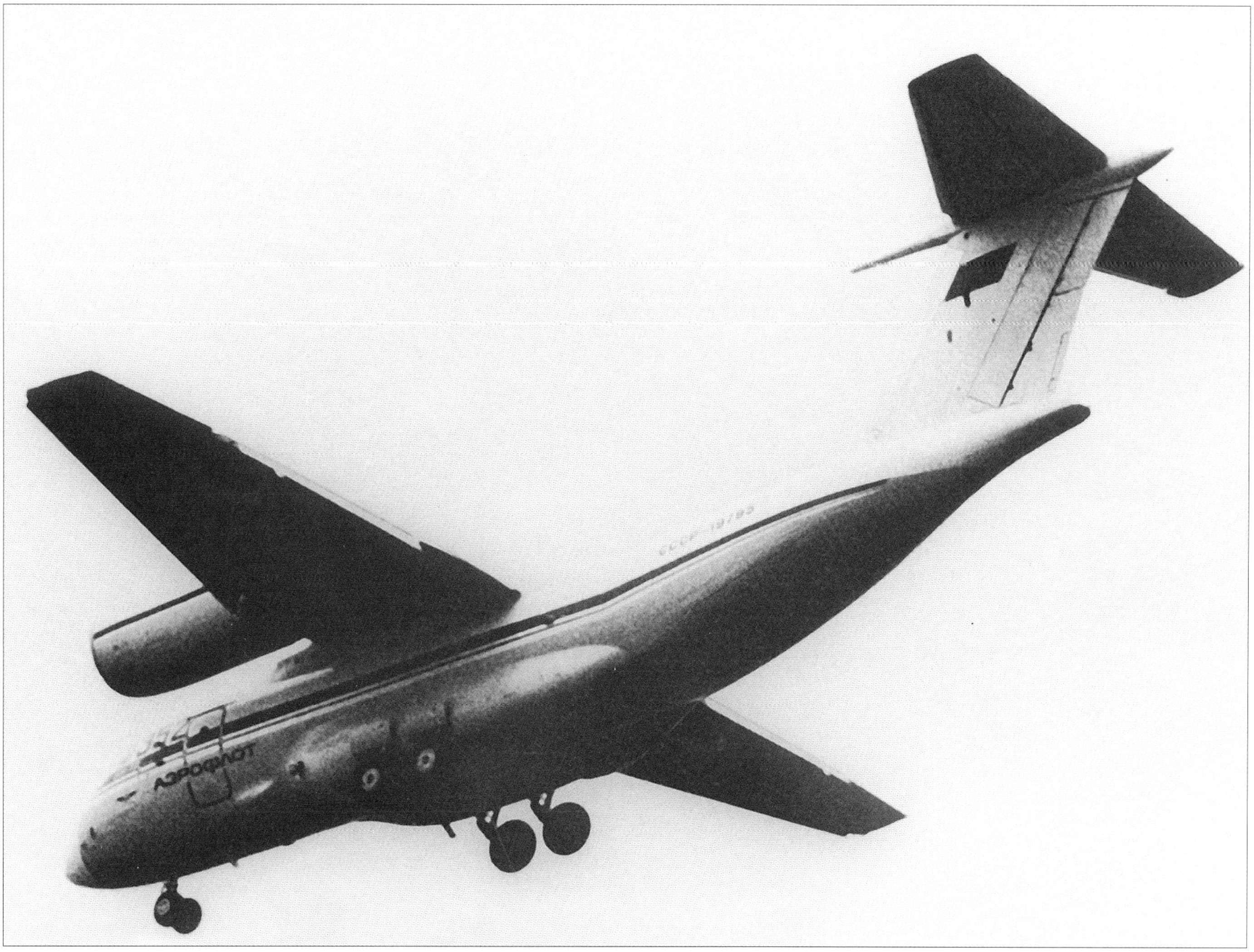

Top and above: The third prototype An-72 makes a demonstration flight at Le Bourget '81.

Above: Later, An-72 CCCP-19795 was reregistered CCCP-72000 to underscore the type. This shot illustrates the operation of the An-72's bucket-type thrust reversers.

banked turns, low-speed passes and, as the cherry on the cake, a 'pinpoint' landing with a very short landing run. (This was later excelled by another An-72, but that was a modified example with a specially reinforced airframe for airshow antics.) After the type's Le Bourget appearance the NATO's Air Standards Co-ordinating Committee (ASCC) assigned the singularly undignified reporting name *Coaler* to the An-72.

In late 1979 the An-72 was submitted for state acceptance trials. The main customer (the Soviet Air Force) was so satisfied with the aircraft's performance that it did not even draw up the so-called 'list No.1' (the customary list of deficiencies to be rectified as soon as possible)! This was almost unheard-of in Soviet aviation history.

A few words have to be said here on the fate of the three prototypes mentioned above. The first prototype (CCCP-83966 No.2) was reregistered again, becoming CCCP-72004. It was subsequently wrecked in a landing accident at Kiev-Gostomel' but later rebuilt as the first prototype An-71 AWACS aircraft. CCCP-19793 was converted less extensively to become the prototype of the An-72A (An-74), described in Chapter 2, and reregistered CCCP-780334. The third prototype, CCCP-19795, became CCCP-72000 and was eventually retired.

decision to launch full-scale production of the new aircraft was taken even before the An-72 had completed its trials programme. However, the An-72 was not destined to enter production in as-was condition…

On 12th-19th May 1979 the first prototype An-72 made its international debut at the 33rd Paris Air Show at Le Bourget, bearing the exhibit code 350 and the legend *Eksperimen**tahl'**nyy* (Experimental). The aircraft, which had by then received a new 'MAP-style' registration CCCP-83966 (the 839xx batch was one of those used by MAP), was already *sans* strakes and featured the revised tailcone, rudder and fin bullet fairing but still retained the old cargo door design. The registration had been reused, having been originally worn by an early-production An-26 (c/n 1006) belonging to the Antonov OKB; this aircraft was subsequently converted to the first prototype An-32, and the registration was later freed up when CCCP-83966 No.1 was reregistered CCCP-46961 and converted into the An-32LL propfan technology testbed.

The An-72 drew considerable attention at Le Bourget by virtue of its unconventional layout and its high performance. The high thrust/weight ratio reaching 0.42 at normal take-off weight, coupled with the high wing loading, enabled the new Antonov transport to put on a spectacular display, demonstrating quite unexpected agility for a transport aircraft. The demonstration flight included a short take-off followed by a steep climb, 45°

The original intention was to launch An-72 production at the Kiev Aircraft Production Association (KiAPO – ***Kiy**evskoye aviatsi**on**noye proiz**vod**stvennoye obyedi**neni**ye*), alias MAP plant No.473, at Kiev-Svyatoshino – right next door to the OKB. The close proximity of the OKB would be invaluable, allowing the problems which inevitably crop up during the learning curve to be resolved quickly. Actually preparations for series production did get under way in 1978; the necessary

An-72 CCCP-72000 parked at Farnborough.

Above: An-72 CCCP-72000 makes a turn with the flaps fully deployed and the cargo ramp in paradropping position (under the belly)

CCCP-72000 shares the north ramp at Farnborough with two Dornier 228s (including an Air Botswana example), a Saab-Fairchild SF340A demonstrator and a Royal Navy Westland Sea King HAS.Mk 3.

manufacturing documents were prepared, jigs and tooling were manufactured, and workforce training was in progress. However, KiAPO had no spare capacity at the time, being busy manufacturing the An-32 which enjoyed considerable export success; mastering production of one more type embodying a lot of new technology could jeopardise the An-32 production and delivery plans.

Meanwhile, not too far away, production of the Tupolev Tu-134 short/medium-haul airliner was drawing to a close at the Khar'kov Aircraft Production Association (KhAPO – *Khar'kovskoye aviatsionnoye proizvodstvennoye obyedineniye*), aka MAP plant No.135. This plant could be freed up for An-72 production. This scenario suited the Antonov OKB just fine – both of the two production aircraft factories located in the Ukraine would be at the OKB's disposal; General Designer Oleg K. Antonov, who visited Khar'kov on numerous occasions, was quoted as saying, *'as General Designer I would like to see my aircraft produced at this plant'*.

The management of KhAPO, on the other hand, was not overjoyed about this prospect; the plant was a long-standing Tupolev partner, and a transition to Antonov aircraft would mean a total change of technology. Therefore the plant's management urged MAP to 'pick some Tupolev design for them to build'. Yet, after much lobbying and infighting an MAP decision was taken and it could not be overruled. KhAPO was ordered to start tooling up for An-72 production and deliver the first production aircraft in 1983. The Kiev plant began transferring all the numerous documents and jigs to Khar'kov.

The An-72 was designed as a multi-role aircraft suitable for transporting and paradropping various cargoes and personnel; to this end the cargo handling equipment included a travelling hoist of 2,500 kg (5,510 lb) capacity and removable roller tracks on the freight hold floor. The navigation and communications suites enabled precision navigation along airways and pre-programmed routes in automatic mode, day and night, in any kind of weather. The spacious flightdeck offered a good field of view on a par with the best Western aircraft in the same class and well laid-out instruments. The field of view and data presentation systems (including a master warning panel) allowed safe navigation into 'beastly' airfields with short runways confined by obstacles, which required steep descent (subsequently known as a 'tactical approach') and steep climbout.

The airframe featured welded/bonded panels with a total area of 150 m^2 (1,613 sq ft), bonded joints with a total area of 70 m^2 (752 sq ft) and riveted/bonded joints with a total length of 284 m (931 ft 9 in). Bonded sandwich panels have a ten times longer service life as compared to chemically milled panels and require 15-20% fewer man-hours to manufacture. Welded/bonded joints are twice as strong and resistant to fatigue as traditional ones and give a weight saving of 5-10%; they are also better sealed against leaks and give a better surface finish.

The An-72 surpassed the transport potential of the twin-turboprop Fiat (Aeritalia) G.222 by 40% and had five times the transport potential of the An-26. An indication of the An-72's capabilities came in 1983 when test pilots Marina L. Popovich and Sergey Maksimov set two world altitude records – 13,410 m (43,996 ft) in a zoom climb and 12,980 m (42,585 ft) in sustained level flight. Two years later Antonov OKB test pilot Sergey A. Gorbik averaged 681.8 km/h (423.47 mph) in an An-72 over a 2,000-km (1,242-mile) closed circuit.

The Ministry of Civil Aviation – that is, the sole Soviet airline, Aeroflot – also evinced an interest in the promising new airlifter, being in need of a replacement for its obsolescent fleet of An-26s and An-12s. A STOL transport suited to harsh operating conditions was just the right recipe for the remote regions of the High North, Siberia and the Soviet Far East, where small towns and weather research stations in the middle of nowhere usually had only limited airfield facilities. However, Aeroflot's operational requirements were quite different from the military specification to which the An-72 had been designed. The airline was not going to accept a 'short-legged' aircraft with a payload of only 5 tons; thus, the MGA demanded that the aircraft should have a range of at least 3,200 km (1,987 miles) with a normal payload and 2-hour fuel reserves. Also, the MGA wanted twice the An-72's normal payload – that is, 10 tons (22,040 lb).

The Antonov OKB found itself in a predicament. Reconciling the contradictory requirements of the commercial and military customers involved a major redesign, and the big question was how to do it. Merely increasing the fuel capacity was a 'quick fix' – this would increase the wing loading and reduce the thrust/weight ratio, ruining the aircraft's STOL capability. The designers opted for a compromise solution – the wing area and aspect ratio were to be increased, leaving the rest of the airframe unchanged. The original intention was to mate all-new outer wings to the existing wing centre section. However, the obsolete machine tools with which KhAPO was then equipped could not handle the required one-piece milled skin panels whose length reached 12 m (39 ft 4 in).

The solution arrived at eventually was another 'quick fix' – the designers simply lopped off the outer portions of the existing wings in line with the flaps' outer ends and grafted on new outer wings to achieve the desired area, introducing two more manufacturing breaks into the wing structure. The wing area increased from 89.6 m^2 (963.4 sq ft) to 98.78 m^2 (1,062.1 sq ft) and the aspect ratio from 7.4 to 11.2. The redesigned wing torsion box incorporated additional tankage, bringing the total fuel capacity to 16,250 litres (3,575 Imp gal).

The modification changed the wing planform perceptibly, leading-edge sweep being reduced and trailing-edge sweep introduced outboard of the inner/outer wing joints. The ailerons were split into inner and outer sections to prevent aeroelasticity problems, the inboard sections (assisted by spoilers) being used in cruise flight and the outer sections joining in at low speeds. Fixed trailing edge portions were introduced outboard of the ailerons.

The requested increase in freight hold length and volume was achieved by inserting a 1.4-m (4 ft 7$\frac{7}{64}$ in) 'plug' with three additional fuselage frames into the forward fuselage aft of the entry door. This fuselage stretch also eliminated the tendency to side-slip characteristic of aircraft with high aspect ratio wings and, as a bonus, gave the An-72 more elegant proportions.

This made it possible to quickly modify some of the prototypes at the OKB's Kiev facility. One of them was c/n 003, which became the An-74 prototype in the process; the other one was c/n 006. This aircraft is something of a mystery. There are reasons to believe it never flew as a short-wing/short-fuselage prototype and was converted as the pattern aircraft for An-72 production. This aircraft was later converted as the prototype of the An-72P border patrol version.

Tests of the redesigned An-72 showed that maximum range had increased to 5,000 km (3,105 miles), or 4,200 km (2,609 miles) with a 1.5-ton (3,310-lb) payload and two-hour fuel reserves. On the minus side, the fuselage stretch and the larger wings led to an increase in empty weight. Also, the wing aerodynamics were far from perfect, the leading- and trailing-edge kinks at the inner/outer wing joints generating harmful vortices which induced drag. As a result, maximum speed dropped from 720 to 705 km/h (from 447 to 437 mph), while the cruising speed was reduced even more dramatically from 650 to 530-550 km/h (from 403 to 329-341 mph), equalling that of the propeller-driven An-32.

The Coanda effect now accounted for only 5-7% of the wing lift, most of the lift being provided by the larger wings. The four spoilers (airbrakes) on the wing centre section were deleted, as tests had shown them to be ineffective – the airbrakes were blanked out by the engine nacelles during the landing approach. Changes were also made to the flight and navigation avionics suite.

Chapter 2

Coaler & Co.

The Twinjet Family

This chapter deals with the production An-72 and its production and experimental versions, some of which bore different designations.

An-72 light military transport (*izdeliye* 72)

In August 1981 MAP approved the schedule according to which technology transfer to KhAPO and preparations for An-72 production were to proceed, setting the deadline when the first Khar'kov-built production example was to be manufactured. A team of KhAPO engineers headed by project engineer V. P. Velik accepted the manufacturing documents. Technology issues were handled by the plant's chief technologist V. I. Zayats and his deputy A. Ye. Mironov.

This is where KhAPO ran into the first problems associated with the An-72 (or *izdeliye* 72, as it was appropriately coded at the plant; *izd**el**iye* (product) such-and-such is a term often used for coding Soviet/Russian military hardware items). To begin with, the manufacturing documents were divided into two categories – the 'frozen' ones (that is, for the components that were 'inherited' from the original short-fuselage/short-wing prototype configuration) and the altered ones. The first category included the tail unit, landing gear, engine nacelles and some other components which remained unchanged; the second category included the fuselage with its 1.4-m (4 ft 7⁷⁄₆₄ in) stretch and longer recontoured radome, the larger-span wings with their additional manufacturing breaks, redesigned high-lift devices and ailerons, and so on.

KhAPO received the manufacturing documents from two plants at once – the Kiev Mechanical Plant (KMZ – ***Ki**yevskiy mekha-**ni**cheskiy za**vod***), as the Antonov OKB was referred to in unclassified correspondence at the time, and KiAPO; both of them had been involved in An-72 prototype construction and modification. It quickly turned out that the drawings supplied by KiAPO included an awful lot of temporary (and contradictory) documents incorporating last-minute changes and were, for all practical purposes, unfit for working with. The reason was plain – KiAPO had been commissioned to build another type (the An-124) and was in a hurry to get rid of the An-72. Thus, in spite of the Khar'kov engineers' protests, the plant was given a half-baked product which took a lot of time and effort to put right.

The controversial 'inheritance' was not limited to the drawings. The documents were followed by the numerous templates, jigs and tools which the OKB's experimental shop and the production plant in Kiev had used for manufacturing the prototypes. These were also thick with faults and inaccuracies; in prototype construction it was sometimes easier to 'cut and bend to shape' than to spend time finding out why the size of a given part had gone wrong. However, what worked in prototype construction was no good for mass production. It took literally years to weed out all the many mismatches in the design documentation and adapt it to the actual conditions of mass production in Khar'kov – and, understandably, this did not help to speed up the An-72's production entry a bit.

As was customary in the Soviet Union, one delay led to others; design difficulties and technological bugs immediately generated organisational problems in which the entire factory gradually bogged down. Transitioning from large-scale production of a well-mastered design to a totally new product is always a challenge, especially when the new product is a state-of-the-art aircraft with its multitude of components, many of which are subcontracted out. The Khar'kov Aircraft Production Association's chief engineer L. P. Vasil'-chenko, chief designer N. G. Yanat'yev, his deputies A. M. Min'kov and N. M. Panchenko, chief technologist V. I. Zayats and chief metallurgist V. I. Bok shouldered a huge load of responsibility, preparing all of the plant's many subdivisions for the difficult transition to the new product.

Panchenko, who was project engineer for the An-72 programme, recalls that *'a coordination team was formed to supervise the An-72's introduction. Lots of organisational issues had to be addressed – the procurement of structural materials, off-the-shelf components, stamped parts and so on. New materials were used – with the An-72 we had our first experience of working with titanium and started making large-scale use of composites, large stamped parts and monolithic milled panels. The programme was so important that MAP drafted orders concerning*

An An-72 fuselage being mated with the with the wing centre section at the Khar'kov aircraft factory.

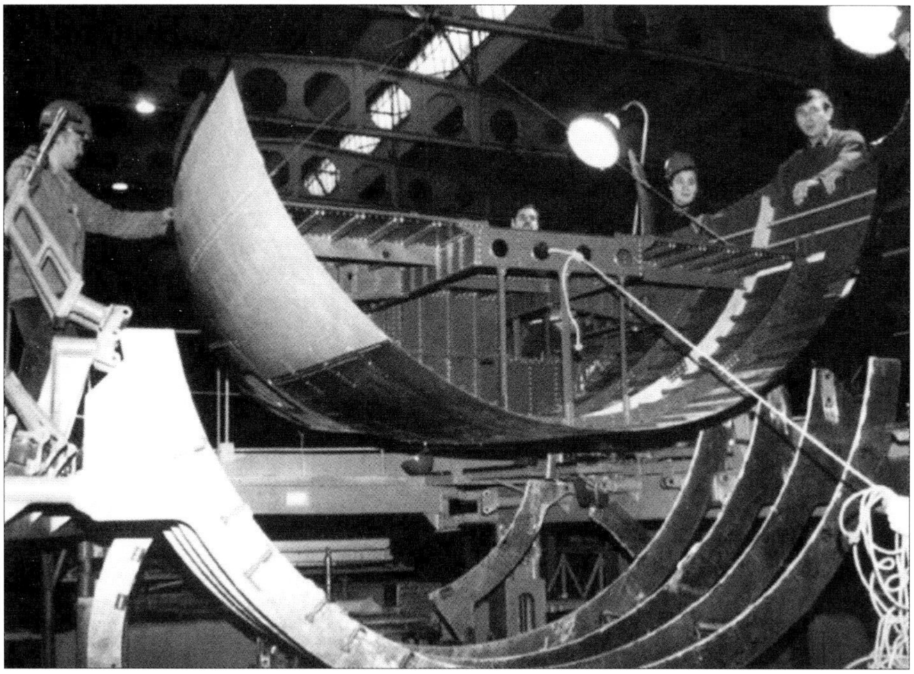

Above: A section of the lower fuselage incorporating the freight hold floor is taken out of the assembly jig for delivery to the centre fuselage build-up area. Note the overhead lamps facilitating quality control.

Above: The An-72's complete wing structure is lifted by an overhead crane. The leading-edge slats are already in place. Note the fuel tank inspection holes.

Assembly workers wearing hard hats inspect the manufacturing joint between the rear fuselage and the unpressurised aft fuselage (tailcone).

materiel deliveries [to KhAPO]. Virtually all of MAP's departments were involved.'

In the preceding years the transition from Tu-104 production to the Tu-124, and especially from the latter to the Tu-134, was facilitated by the Tupolev machines' considerable structural and technological commonality. Now the plant had to deal with a totally different design style – the Antonov OKB's design philosophy was markedly different from those of the Tupolev OKB. So was the manufacturing technology; the An-72 incorporated a host of features which were quite alien to the Khar'kov factory until then. One could justifiably say that after decades of producing Tupolev aircraft, which were quite conservative in their design, the plant had been overtaken by the progress of aviation technology, and now was the time to catch up with it. Mastering new technologies was going to be a tremendous task – all the more so because some of KhAPO's machine tools were pre-World War Two equipment obtained in 1945 from Germany by way of war reparations.

The composite components are a case in point. There were no fewer than 430 parts made of composites in the An-72's airframe, and their aggregate weight was close to 1,000 kg (2,200 lb). Apart from radomes, KhAPO had no prior experience with composite structures. Under the guidance of project engineers V. S. Sivokozov, V. A. Peskov, V. N. Mirnyy, M. B. Tkachov and L. P. Shagayev the factory had to master new technologies. These included impregnation of fillers with resins, manufacturing large integral composite structures forming the exterior of the aircraft, using sandwich-type composite panels instead of chemically milled ones, manufacturing honeycomb structures with various fillers (metal foil, polymer film or glassfibre) and skins (metal, CFRP or organic plastics) and monolithic CFRP and organic plastic components.

The difficulties associated with the new technologies were compounded by materiel procurement problems. For instance, manufacture of CFRP components (landing gear doors, rear cargo door, avionics bay covers and hinged access panels on the wing leading and trailing edge undersides) was delayed a full year because the Soviet Union's State Planning Agency (Gosplan) responsible for economic planning had neglected to order the required carbon fibre from the Soviet chemical industry in a timely fashion.

When Ivan S. Silayev, the then Minister of Aircraft Industry, visited KhAPO in May 1982, he categorically demanded that the first production An-72 be completed before 1st January 1983. Yet, even if the plant's personnel were to do their utmost, this was a Mission Impossible. Firstly, the Tu-134 was still in production (mass production of the type ended in September 1984, but assembly of the Tu-134SKh agricultural survey version continued at a trickle, and the final example was not released by the factory until July 1989). This meant that considerable resources were still committed to the Tu-134 and much of the shop floor space was still allotted to it; built immediately after the war, the assembly shops of the Khar'kov aircraft factory No.135 were simply not designed with large aircraft in mind. Secondly, incessant alterations were being introduced into the design at this stage in accordance with the numerous bulletins and new drawings issued by the Antonov OKB. Hence most of the jigs and tooling received from Kiev, and also those already manufactured on site, became unusable and had to be thrown out. This, of course, led to further delays.

Conversely, in areas where KhAPO did not depend on other plants and institutions, the preparations to build the An-72 were going ahead as planned. For instance, Building 8B was completed in 1982 and all chemical processing of aluminium alloy parts was concentrated within these new premises. The chemical treatment facility featured six fully automatic and semi-automatic processing lines for electrochemical coating, chemical milling and chemical treatment of welded/bonded joints. KhAPO's design and technology departments had significantly amended the original project and, as eventually commissioned, Building 8B was a really state-of-the-art facility having no equal in the Soviet aircraft industry at the time. It featured unique and highly automated and mechanised production lines; delivery of half-finished articles from the warehouse and their processing were controlled by computer programmes. As a result, the quality of the finished product and the working conditions in the hazardous chemical processing areas were greatly improved.

Due to the redesign undertaken to meet Aeroflot requirements and the various associated problems the An-72 became the holder of a controversial 'record', eight years and four months elapsing between the maiden flight and production entry. The first production An-72 (c/n 365.720.10.905, fuselage number 0101) finally took to the air at Khar'kov-Sokol'nikovo on 22nd December 1985, three years later than intended. Originally the aircraft was in grey Air Force colours with star insignia but no tactical code; later it was coded '11 Red'. The first production example was retained by the OKB.

Above: Assembly workers and foremen pose beside the freshly completed but as-yet unpainted first Khar'kov-built An-72 on 26th October 1985.

KhAPO executives and workers pose with the first production An-72 (c/n 365.720.10.905, f/n 0101) at Khar'kov-Sokol'nikovo after its first flight on 20th December 1985. Antonov OKB General Designer Pyotr V. Balabuyev is ninth from left and KhAPO Director A. K. Myalitsa is eleventh from left.

Above: An-72 c/n 365.720.10.905 makes a low pass over the factory airfield, with at least five Aeroflot Tu-134As and one Soviet Air Force Tu-134UBL awaiting delivery visible in the background. The aircraft is light grey overall, with a darker grey radome.

A note must be made here on An-72/An-74 construction numbers. Two systems were used, one for each factory. For many years Khar'kov-built examples had 11-digit c/ns. For instance, An-72 CCCP-72980 manufactured on 16th July 1992 is c/n 365.720.95.909 (this split presentation with dots is often used in official files), explained as follows. 365 is a code for the Khar'kov aircraft factory No.135. This code was possibly obtained by 'doctoring' the factory's number:

(135) 1 – is multiplied by the number of digits in the factory number: 1 x 3 = 3

3 – is multiplied by its sequence number (second digit): 3 x 2 = 6

5 – is left unchanged: 5 (365)

The next three digits are an in-house product code (in this case, 720 = *izdeliye* 72; a zero is added to keep the normally used three-digit format). The remaining five digits do not signify *anything at all*; the idea of this trick devised in 1973 is to confuse would-be spies so that the c/n would not reveal how many aircraft have been built.

Additionally, An-72s and Khar'kov-built An-74s have four-digit *fuselage numbers* (f/ns); security is all very well but the manufacturer has to keep track of production, after all. Typically of Soviet aircraft, the f/n is not just a sequential line number (as in the case of Boeing and Douglas aircraft) but consists of a batch number and the number of the aircraft in the batch; the abovementioned An-72 CCCP-72980 is f/n 1410.

Other versions have different product codes which are duly reflected in the c/n. Thus, An-74 CCCP-74000 manufactured on 31st August 1990 is c/n 365.470.60.649 and f/n 0609, while An-72P CCCP-72908 is c/n 365.760.94.880 and f/n 1303. The first three batches consisted of five aircraft each, the number increasing to ten from Batch 4 onwards. Different civil and military versions are often mixed within a single batch.

As with nearly all Soviet using the 'counter-espionage c/n system', the first two and the last three of the 'famous last five' digits change independently. Oddly, in batches 6 through 17 the first two digits of the 'famous

Three complete early-production An-72 fuselages taken out of the assembly jigs in KhAPO's assembly shop No.27 around 1986. The structure in the assembly jig in the foreground is the upper centre fuselage shell of a Tu-134SKh with cutouts for navigation system sensors in the roof.

last five' add up to show the batch number. Well, it seems the guys at the Khar'kov aircraft factory got carried away, letting the c/ns grow too quickly (maybe they simply didn't count on the An-72/An-74 having a large production run?). Then, realising they were about to run out of numbers in the current system (the two groups of digits were approaching 99 and 999 respectively), they slowed the 'growth rate' to a minimum. Still, by 1999 they *did* run out of numbers.

As with the IL-76, both the first two and the last three digits accrue continuously – since Batch 3 anyway (unlike some other types where the last three digits often drop sharply when the preceding two change, and then start growing again). However, unlike the IL-76, the c/n does not indicate the year of certification and hence starting the two groups from 01 and 000 respectively all over again was impossible. Hence the number of digits in the c/ns was increased to 12 in Batch 20 and then to 13 in Batch 21; for example, An-74TK-100 RA-74016 manufactured on 2nd October 2000 is c/n 365.470.99.1034 and f/n 2007, while the latest known Khar'kov-built example (An-74 15-2261 of the Iranian Revolutionary Guard) is c/n 365.470.121.1059 and f/n 2106.

Omsk-built An-74s have eight-digit c/ns; for instance, RA-74050 manufactured on 21st April 1994 is c/n 47181011. The first two digits are the product code (*izdeliye* 47), the third digit is always a 1 and may denote 'version 1'.

High-ranking MAP and Soviet Air Force officials watch the pre-delivery test flight of an An-72 at Khar'kov-Sokol'nikovo in 1986; other An-72s in Air Force colours are visible beyond.

An uncoded Soviet Air Force An-72 (c/n 365.720.10.952, f/n 0204) at Moscow-Tushino where it was making a series of demonstration flights in 1989; it was later sold to Enimex as ES-NOC. The f/n is painted on the intake covers. On most production aircraft only the tip of the radome is dark grey. Note the open APU intake.

Above: Minister of Aircraft Industry Ivan S. Silayev (second from right) discusses the An-72's production entry schedule with Pyotr V. Balabuyev (second from left) and the then Director of KhAPO Boris A.Khokhlov (rightmost) in 1982. Silayev states a deadline of 1983; the other men are smiling in a 'get real' sort of way.

The significance of the next two digits is unknown, while the last three probably mean Batch 01, first aircraft in the batch.

Khar'kov-built examples usually have the c/n embossed on a small metal plate riveted to the inside of the emergency exit cover at the rear of the cargo cabin, though some aircraft carry the f/n there instead and some lack this plate altogether, which means the c/n is found elsewhere. Also, the c/n (or f/n) is often stencilled on the engine air intake/exhaust and APU exhaust covers, static port covers and 'remove before flight' strips attached to pitot heads. (Spotters beware, though: these may be 'borrowed' from another aircraft; fortunately this is rare.)

The initial production An-72s underwent extensive evaluation in various climatic zones; this included rigorous 'cold soak' trials in Yakutia, the coldest region in the USSR, and 'hot and high' performance testing in the Soviet Union's southern republics. The results of these tests allowed the aircraft's operational envelope to be expanded. In maximum take-off weight (overload) configuration the An-72 grossed at 43 tons (94,800 lb); test pilots noted that the aircraft became sluggish at this weight, and MTOW operations were only authorised for highly experienced pilots.

The baseline An-72 became the progenitor of a whole family of aircraft optimised for widely varying roles. These are described below.

In recent years some Russian Air Force An-72s, including RA-72991 (c/n unknown), were retrofitted with infra-red countermeasures (IRCM) equipment comprising two streamlined fairings on the centre fuselage sides, each of which housed twelve 32-round chaff/

The An-72 final assembly shop at KhAPO. The aircraft are angled to maximise the use of the shop floor space. Note the cargo cabin's dorsal evacuation hatch immediately ahead of the fin and the annular fixtures around the engines on the foremost aircraft to which the cowling doors are hinged.

Top and above: An-72 (c/n 365.720.10.952, f/n 0204) taxying at Moscow-Tushino in 1989.

Above: An-72S RA-72930 (c/n 365.720.70.678, f/n 0702) at Chkalovskaya AB during the ‘open house’ on 15th August 1999 on occasion of Aviation Day. This example represents the all-passenger version.

Another view of the same aircraft. Most of the Soviet/Russian Air Force An-72s were, and still are, quasi-civil. Note the position of the forward IFF aerial on top of the radome.

flare dispenser modules. These fired 26-mm (1.02-in) PPI-26 magnesium flares (PPI = *peeropat**ron** infra**krahs**nyy* – infra-red [countermeasures] cartridge) to decoy infra-red homing missiles. The upgrade was performed by the Russian Air Force's Aircraft Overhaul Plant No.308 at Ivanovo-Severnyy AB.

An-72S VIP aircraft

The first derivative of the production-standard An-72 was a VIP version for the Soviet Ministry of Defence designated An-72S (*salon*; the word has several meanings in Russian, including 'passenger cabin' on an aircraft, but *samo**lyot**-sa**lon*** is the term for 'VIP aircraft'). Actually there were two such versions. On both varieties the forward portion of the freight hold was outfitted as a cabin for the VIPs (referred to as the main passengers), featuring two comfortable seats with a table in between to port and a sofa for three to starboard, airliner-style wall trim and overhead lights. A solid bulkhead with a double door separated the VIP cabin from the rear portion of the hold, which was either left in as-is condition to accommodate a staff car (a GAZ-24 Volga sedan or an UAZ-469 (later redesignated UAZ-3151) jeep) or outfitted as a 20-seat cabin for the retinue, featuring five rows of seats four-abreast with a central aisle. With very few windows, the cabins of the An-72S are not the best of environments for someone prone to claustrophobia! Additional oxygen bottles were installed up on the cabin roof at the rear end.

Known examples include CCCP-72917, CCCP-72930, CCCP-72938, CCCP-72939, CCCP-72942, CCCP-72949 (later Russian Air Force '949 Black') and Russian Air Force '01 Red' (c/n unknown). The first two aircraft in the list are in all-passenger configuration.

The VIP cabin of An-72S RA-72930, with two chairs and a map table on the port side; a sofa for three is located on the other side of the cabin.

An-72-100 commercial cargo aircraft

Lately some An-72s have been sold to civil operators and demilitarised by replacing some of the avionics (including communications radios with different frequency grids). Such aircraft are designated An-72-100. Known examples are registered RA-72936 (c/n 365.720.60.642, f/n 0607), ES-NOC (c/n 365.720.10.952, f/n 0204), ES-NOG (ex-RA-72942, c/n 365.720.80.786, f/n 0807) and ES-NOK (ex-RA-72939, c/n 365.720.80.780, f/n 0804).

An-72-100D commercial cargo/executive aircraft

A similarly demilitarised version featuring a VIP interior is designated An-72-100D, the D standing for *de**lo**voy* – executive or business, used attributively. So far only one example, RA-72982 (c/n 365.720.96.914, f/n 1503), has been identified; this aircraft was sold abroad to become 3C-QQO and then ES-NOI.

An-72PS SAR aircraft (project)

A maritime search and rescue version designated An-72PS (*pois**ko**vo-spa**sah**tel'nyy* – SAR, used attributively) was under development for the Soviet Naval Aviation. The aircraft's intended mission was to locate Navy or civilian ships in distress or downed aircraft and extend help by paradropping life rafts and other materiel, as well as rescue teams.

An-72 ASW aircraft (project)

Another projected naval version of the An-72 was a shore-based anti-submarine warfare aircraft with a towed magnetic anomaly detector (MAD) 'bird'. No information is available as to what weapons the aircraft was to carry, and how.

An-72 firebomber (project)

A purely civil version of the An-72 was intended for fighting forest fires which occur in the thickly wooded eastern regions of the Soviet Union, and now Russia, with uncanny regularity. Due to the An-72's main landing gear arrangement it was obviously impossible to carry the water or fire retardant in external tanks scabbed on to the fuselage sides, as was the case with the An-26P and An-32P Firekiller (the P suffix stood for *po**zhar**nyy* – firefighting, used attributively). The water tanks could only be installed in the freight hold to discharge through the cargo door after the cargo ramp had been opened. This made the aircraft readily convertible from transport to waterbomber and back but made it impossible to carry a crew of firefighters to be paradropped into the area. Perhaps it was this, or possibly the pressure of higher-priority programmes, that led the project to be shelved – unlike the An-32P.

An-72 flying boat derivative (project)

Probably the most ambitious project based on the An-72 envisaged turning the landplane transport into a cargo flying boat (or possibly an amphibian) featuring a totally new fuselage with a side cargo door and outrigger floats under the wingtips. This was, in a way, the forebear of the Beriyev Be-200 multi-role twin-turbofan amphibian.

An-72 COD aircraft (project)

As the Soviet Navy strove to build up a fleet of conventional take-off and landing (CTOL) aircraft carriers in order to match the carrier capability of the Western navies, several Soviet aircraft design bureaux were ordered to start work on CTOL shipboard aircraft. Of course, these were primarily combat aircraft, but the projects of aircraft intended for the Soviet Navy's new carriers included a version of the An-72 optimised for carrier on-board delivery (COD) duties – the Soviet counterpart of the Lockheed US-3A Viking.

Above and below: The first prototype of the An-72R ELINT/ECM aircraft (presumably c/n 365.720.10.912, f/n 0103) withdrawn from use at Kiev-Svyatoshino, sitting in plain view of the visitors of the third Aviasvit-XXI airshow (18th-21st September 2004). Note the shape of the huge antenna fairings.

Above and below: The starboard antenna fairing obstructs the emergency exit; the two rearmost dielectric panels on this side are still in place. Note the ventral dielectric fairing ahead of the main gear fairing. Unlike later examples, the first prototype An-72R retains the standard vertical tail.

Above: The other three An-72R prototypes were quasi-civil; also, they featured a large fin fillet and reshaped lateral antenna fairings. The third prototype, CCCP-783573 (also coded ‘38 Red’; c/n 365.720.10.935, f/n 0105) is seen here at Vladimirovka AB, Akhtoobinsk.

The fourth and final example (CCCP-784072/‘39 Red’, c/n 365.720.10.940, f/n 0201) shows off the reshaped (more angular) rear portions of the antenna fairings.

The intended role necessitated major structural changes. Firstly, the aircraft featured folding wings to save deck space so as not to hamper the operations of other aircraft while it was on deck. Secondly, the landing gear would obviously have to be redesigned, with beefed-up long-stroke oleos enabling no-flare landings characteristic of CTOL carrier operations and, in view of the An-72's high weight, permitting launch by steam catapult. Thirdly, the entire airframe would need to be reinforced to absorb the higher loads.

Eventually only a single CTOL carrier, the SNS *Tbilisi*, entered service with the Soviet Navy (she is now in service with the Russian North Fleet as the RNS *Admiral Kuznetsov*). The larger SNS *Ul'yanovsk* was never completed and the requirement for a COD aircraft based on the An-72 died with her.

An-72 CASEVAC version

The basic An-72 transport could be quickly adapted for casualty evacuation (CASEVAC) duties. Several tiers of stretchers were fixed to uprights and straps in the freight hold to accommodate up to 24 casualties, with a seat for a medical attendant at the front of the hold. The CASEVAC kit was optional and could be supplied together with the aircraft.

At least one such aircraft saw service with the 8th ADON (*aviadi**vee**ziya o**sob**ovo naz-na**chen**iya* – Special Mission Air Division, ≈ air wing) at Chkalovskaya AB. It could carry a maximum of 29 casualties, including eight stretcher cases; the stretchers were located in the rear portion of the hold to minimise loading/unloading time, while walking wounded could be seated in the centre portion of the hold. A bunk, a table and two seats at the front were provided for the medics. Intensive care equipment, including a lung ventilation apparatus, was also provided, as was a supply of medicines, intravenous kits and disposable syringes. Thus, in spite of the somewhat cramped cabin, it was possible to extend first aid in flight to seriously wounded personnel.

An-72R ELINT/ECM aircraft (*izdeliye* 88?)

Development of an electronic intelligence (ELINT) and active electronic countermeasures (ECM) version of the An-72 began in the early 1980s while KhAPO was still gearing up to build the baseline model. Originally the ELINT/ECM version was to have been designated An-72P (*posta**nov**schchik po**mekh*** – ECM aircraft); some sources call it *izdeliye* 88. Later, however, the An-72P designation was reassigned to an armed patrol version (see below) and *izdeliye* 88 came to be known as the An-72R ([*samo**lyot***] ***rah**diotekh**nich**eskoy raz**ved**ki* – ELINT aircraft). The ELINT version is sometimes referred to in Western publications as the An-73.

Four prototypes of the An-72R were converted from four consecutively built initial-production airframes. The ELINT/ECM version featured large slab-sided conformal antenna fairings with faired front and rear ends running almost the full length of the fuselage; they incorporated several dielectric panels each and widened at the rear (in side view, that is) where they flanked the cargo ramp. The starboard fairing obscured the emergency exit, which had to be eliminated, but, since most of the cabin was occupied by mission equipment, the entry door was enough for evacuating the flight crew and equipment operators.

The first prototype (presumably c/n 365.720.10.912, f/n 0103) was painted grey overall and devoid of any markings. Flight tests showed that the antenna fairings generated vortices, impairing the aircraft's directional stability; hence the other prototypes had the vertical tail augmented by a large dorsal fin and the rear ends of the fairings were reshaped. These three aircraft wore full Aeroflot colours and non-standard six-digit registrations augmented by a military tactical code above the Soviet flag (!). Thus, the second prototype was registered CCCP-783061 and coded '37 Red' (c/n 365.720.10.930, f/n 0104), the third aircraft was CCCP-783573/'38 Red' (c/n 365.720.10.935, f/n 0105) and the final example was CCCP-784072/'39 Red' (c/n 365.720.10.940, f/n 0201). Interestingly, the quasi-civil examples carried appropriate 'An-72R' nose titles. (See comment on the six-digit registrations in the An-74 section below.)

The An-72R underwent lengthy trials at the Soviet Air Force State Research Institute named after Valeriy P. Chkalov (GNIKI VVS – *Gosoo**dar**stvennyy na**ooch**no-is**sled**ovatel'-skiy krasnozna**myon**nyy insti**toot** vo**yen**no-voz**doosh**nykh seel*; the word *krasnozna-**myon**nyy* means that the institute was awarded the Order of the Red Banner). Unlike the transport version, which was tested by GNIKI VVS's transport aircraft division at Chkalovskaya AB, the An-72Rs operated from the institute's main facility at Vladimirovka AB in Akhtoobinsk near Saratov, southern Russia. The tests included a near-accident involving CCCP-783061/'37 Red' in April 1987 when one of the thrust reversers deployed uncommandedly on take-off.

After the demise of the Soviet Union most of the Russian Air Force's advanced aircraft programmes had to be mothballed due to funding problems and the fact that many of the component suppliers found themselves outside Russia and new-found sovereignty caused economic co-operation ties to be severed. The An-72R was just one of many aircraft that fell victim to these circumstances. The first prototype, stripped of engines and all mission equipment, could be seen at Kiev-Svyatoshino during the third Aviasvit-XXI airshow (18th-21st September 2004). The other three are probably still in storage in Akhtoobinsk at what is now the 929th GLITs (*Gosoo**dar**stvennyy **lyot**no-ispy**tah**tel'nyy tsentr* – State Flight Test Centre).

An-72P border patrol aircraft (*izdeliye* 76?)

The An-72P designation was reused for another special mission derivative of the *Coaler* – a border patrol aircraft developed to meet a specification drafted by the Border Guards Directorate of the notorious KGB (State Security Committee). Thus, the P suffix now stood for *pat**rool'**nyy* (patrol, used attributively) or *pogra**nich**nyy* (in this case, Border Guards, used attributively).

Since many An-72Ps are now stationed on Russia's Pacific coast, Western observers tend to regard the model as a maritime patrol aircraft, which is not quite correct. Still, the An-72P's range, endurance and payload *does* make it suitable for patrolling the 200-mile economic exclusion zone as much as for patrolling land borders. The aircraft can operate around the clock in fair or adverse weather, cruising or loitering at 500-1,000 m (1,640-3,280 ft) and 300-350 km/h (186-217 mph) for up to 5 hours 20 minutes. With a full 5-ton (11,020-lb) payload, the aircraft has a range of 2,800 km (1,739 miles).

The An-72P is based on the original transport version. Apart from patrolling the border and coastal areas and detecting and following intruders, it can paradrop up to 22 troopers or transport up to 44 fully equipped troops; to this end the pressurised and air-conditioned cabin is provided with removable centreline seats, some of which are attached to the cargo ramp. Alternatively, the aircraft can evacuate up to 16 casualties (stretcher cases) with a medical attendant or transport ammunition and other materiel weighing up to 5 tons.

In view of its mission involving flight over border areas (where accurate navigation was crucial) the An-72P has a crew of five – two pilots, a flight engineer, a navigator and a radio operator/observer. The latter two crewmembers are provided with observation blisters on the port and starboard sides respectively.

The mission equipment includes:

- a flight/navigation/targeting suite enabling automatic flight throughout the mission, a 'go-to' function bringing the machine automatically to a point with pre-entered co-ordinates, search and detection for surface ships. The suite makes it possible to determine the ship's co-ordinates, heading and speed;
- cameras for daytime vertical and oblique photography of ground objects and surface ships, with provisions for recording the co-ordinates of the spot where the picture

Above: A KhAPO test crew poses with the first production An-72P after the first flight. Left to right: V. A. Antonov, Yu. I. Nalivaïko, S. V. Chaïchenko, V. P. Samodoorov, V. Yu. Voylokov, A. I. Koorchenko and V. I. Goobarev.

was taken to provide proof positive of a border violation. Only vertical photography is possible at night, assisted by SFP-2A illumination flares;

• a day/night television surveillance and image recording system;

• a communications suite ensuring two-way metre- and decimetre-waveband and HF/VHF communication with the ground, other aircraft or ships (among other things, for the purpose of guiding patrol boats to intercept an intruding ship);

• armament.

The latter feature deserves special mention. The armament is intended not so much for destroying an intruder (though the An-72P *can* sink a ship if needs must, as was demonstrated on one occasion!) but rather for making it clear even to the most thick-headed or self-assured intruder that he cannot get away. To this end a UPK-23-250 pod (*oonifi**tsee**rovannyy **push**echnyy kon**tey**ner* – standardised gun pod) containing a 23-mm (.90 calibre) Gryazev/Shipoonov GSh-23L double-barrel fast-firing cannon with 250 rounds is carried on an L-shaped pylon ahead of the main gear fairing to starboard, its rear end fitting into a cutout in the fairing's front portion. The cannon's rate of fire is 3,200 rpm.

Two further pylons are fitted under the wings just outboard of the engines for carrying UB-32 pods with thirty-two 57-mm (2.24-in.) S-5 folding-fin aircraft rockets (FFARs) apiece – or bombs of up to 500 kg (1,102 lb) calibre. (UB = *oonifi**tsee**rovannyy blok* – standardised [FFAR] pod; S = *sna**ryad*** – in this case, unguided rocket.) Additionally, four 100-kg (220-lb) bombs can be hooked up to shackles on the freight hold roof (this requires the cargo ramp to be slid forward before they are dropped). The cargo hatch can be used for dropping beacons, buoys or life rafts.

The wing structure is reinforced to enable low-altitude flight in turbulence (which is often encountered over the sea). Later the reinforced wings became a standard feature on all An-72s and An-74s.

The An-72P prototype was converted from the final Kiev-built example (c/n 006) which, as recounted in the previous chapter, was possibly registered CCCP-72002 before that. The modified aircraft received full Soviet Air Force markings, a three-tone camouflage scheme and, some time after the first flight, the tactical code '06 Yellow'.

Production began in 1990. The aircraft made its public debut at Farnborough International '92 when a production example coded '07 Red' (c/n 365.760.96.915, f/n 1504) and wearing a Ukrainian flag was in the static park. The internal bomb stowage astounded the Westerners. As Roy Braybrook, a columnist working for the *Air International* magazine, wrote: *'...we were told* (at an Antonov press conference – *Auth.*) *that four 100-kg (220-lb) bombs could be carried* inside the cargo cabin. *Frankly, I thought that either the interpreter had got it wrong or we really should have declined the SBAC's* kir royales. *How-*

Grey-painted An-72 CCCP-71052 (c/n 365.720.80.775, f/n 0801) pictured at Pushkin airfield near Leningrad appears to be some kind of testbed. It has additional dorsal and ventral aerials and antenna blisters, an An-72P-style observation blister to starboard and apparently a ventral camera port as well but no armament.

Top and above: The An-72P prototype, '06 Yellow' (c/n 006), making a demonstration flight at the MosAeroShow '92. Note the equipment cooling air intake at the base of the fin; this was not incorporated on production aircraft.

Above: The An-72P prototype at Kiev-Svyatoshino in September 2000, now in Ukrainian Air Force markings and wearing 'Antonov 72P' titles and Antonov OKB logos. The additional ventral blade aerials and antenna blisters characteristic of this version are clearly visible. The wing pylons have been removed.

The same aircraft six years earlier at the Asian Aerospace '94 as an Israel Aircraft Industries upgrade demonstrator with an Elta EL/M 2022A radar and an El-Op observation system in a ventral turret.

ever, when we were finally allowed inside the thing, these high-drag stores were there as advertised, just waiting for the pilot to jettison the cargo ramp so that he could go bomb someone! Strange chaps, these Ukrainians.' Well, with all due respect, Mr. Braybrook, sarcasm is a poor substitute for being informed on the An-72's patented cargo ramp design.

Shortly afterwards the An-72P prototype was displayed the MosAeroShow '92 (11th-16th August 1992) in the town of Zhukovskiy, both statically and in flight. The demonstration flights deserve special mention, as the prototype's specially reinforced airframe allowed the crew to make spectacular manoeuvres, including barrel rolls and a half loop. Later this aircraft took part in many international airshows, wearing Ukrainian Air Force insignia.

Production, however, had begun some time before the patrol version's public debut, and about 13 production examples were built. The first of them entered service with Border Guards units stationed in the Soviet Far East. Only one production An-72P (CCCP-72970) was quasi-civil; the rest wore overt military markings (see Chapter 5).

An-72P (Israeli upgrade)

The An-72P prototype was later upgraded by Israel Aircraft Industries in an attempt to enhance its appeal to foreign customers. The avionics fit included digital cockpit avionics, an Elta EL/M 2022A maritime surveillance radar, an El-Op day/night long-range observation system in a ventral revolving turret and an Elisra electronic warfare suite; the aircraft could carry IAI Griffin laser-guided bomb on the wing hardpoints.

The modified An-72P was exhibited at Asian Aerospace '94 at Singapore-Changi between 22nd and 27th February 1994, sporting additional IAI logos. However, nothing came of this project; the Israeli avionics and IAI logos were removed by September 2000.

An-72V light military transport

The designation An-72V has been quoted for three An-72s delivered to Peru. The An-72V probably differed from the domestic version only in avionics fit.

An-72G light military transport

This designation was quoted for a single An-72 belonging to the Antonov ANTK. Registered 72966 (with no nationality prefix; c/n 365.720.92.847, f/n 1104), the aircraft could be identified by the An-72P-style port side observation blisters.

The An-72G gained most unwelcome publicity when it collided with the unregistered first prototype of the An-70 four-propfan medium military transport (c/n 0101) near Kiev-Gostomel' during a test flight on 10th February 1995. The An-70 lost half its tail unit and crashed out of control, killing all on board; this was a severe setback to the An-70 programme whose consequences have not been overcome to this day. The damaged An-72G managed a safe landing at Gostomel' but has been grounded ever since.

An-72G navigation system testbed

A production An-72 coded '03 Red' (c/n 365.720.60.610, f/n 0603) was converted by the Flight Research Institute named after Mikhail M. Gromov (LII – ***Lyot**no-is**sle**dovatel'skiy insti**toot***) in Zhukovskiy for testing advanced automatic landing systems and satellite navigation systems. The aircraft had worn a different tactical code (possibly '24') before transfer to LII.

Outwardly the only non-standard features were two whip aerials in tandem and a small antenna blister ahead of them low on the port side of the forward fuselage. The new avionics and test/data recording equipment were mounted in a small cubicle at the front of the freight hold; a navigation display was installed in the flightdeck. Interestingly, a 'Danger, air intake' warning triangle (a definitely non-standard feature) was applied ahead of the APU air intake. The testbed was displayed statically at the MAKS-97 airshow in Zhukovskiy on 19th-24th August 1997.

Above: An-72 '03 Red' (c/n 365.720.60.610, f/n 0603), a navigation systems testbed, at the MAKS-97 airshow. Note the extra aerials aft of the entry door. The aircraft shows obvious signs of being recoded.

An-72Sh light military transport (project)

An interesting project developed by the Antonov OKB envisaged fitting the An-72 with an air cushion landing gear to improve its ability to operate from unpaved or soggy runways. Designated An-72Sh (the suffix denoted *shas**see*** – landing gear), the aircraft apparently was to have individual air cushion platforms with rubber skirts supplanting the normal landing gear units in the manner of the An-714 testbed. Eventually, however, the project posed insurmountable technical problems and was abandoned.

An-71 AEW&C aircraft

The An-72 served as the basis for a radically redesigned airborne early warning and control aircraft, the An-71. Featuring a highly unusual layout with a rotodome on top of a forward-swept vertical tail (!), this aircraft was intended for both land-based and shipboard operations. The An-71 will be described in the forthcoming book on Soviet/ Russian AWACS aircraft in the Red Star series (Vol.23).

An-72A (An-74) commercial transport (*izdeliye* 72.07, *izdeliye* 47.000)

In December 1980 the Ministry of Aircraft Industry issued order No.519 requiring the Antonov OKB to develop a single basic aircraft (based on the An-72) for military and civil applications within a two-year period. Pursuant to the same document KhAPO was to launch production of this aircraft in 1983.

According to MAP order No.519, operations in Polar regions were to be the aircraft's main civil application. The reason was that Aeroflot had long been clamouring for a commercial transport suitable both for regular services in the High North, where aircraft are

The An-74 prototype (CCCP780334) takes off on an early test flight. The original radome has been substituted with a modified one incorporating a long pointed air data probe, which is standard practice at the Antonov OKB, starting with the An-72. The aircraft is in high-visibility 'Polar' Aeroflot colours

Above: Passing over the nuclear-powered icebreaker N/V *Sibir'*, the An-74 prototype shows off the original short radome, the long ventral strake aerial and the two port side observation blisters of equal size.

Another air-to-air of CCCP-780334 above the broken icefields in the Arctic Ocean, showing to advantage the cranked trailing edge of the new increased-area wings. The colour division lines on the wings coincide with the inner/outer wing panel joints.

Above: The prototype's colour scheme deviated from the 1973-standard red/white 'Polar' Aeroflot livery in more than one way. Note the unusually small Aeroflot titles and the colour division line located halfway up the fin (at the upper/lower rudder segment joint); compare this to later examples.

CCCP-780334 shares the ramp at Kiev-Svyatoshino with an An-32. The flaps and thrust reversers are fully deployed and the cargo ramp is halfway through its travel as it slides forward under the fuselage.

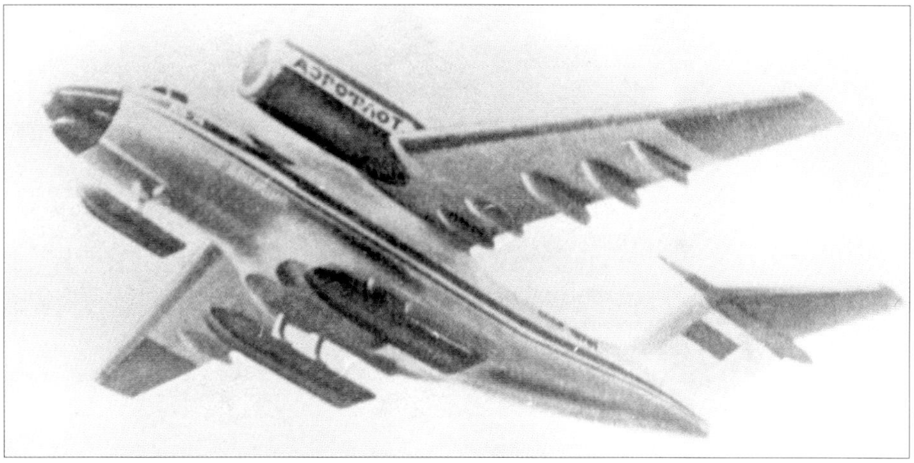

Above: The An-74 was intended to have a retractable ski landing gear, as this model bearing *Polyarnaya Aviatsiya* (Polar Aviation) titles shows. Note the recesses in the main gear fairing and the undernose fairing reminiscent of the Lockheed LC-130F Hercules. The idea never materialised.

Centre and above: Still with its original radome, the An-74 prototype is seen visiting a Soviet airport. Note the retired Tu-114 turboprop airliner used as a fire trainer in the background.

often the sole means of transport and communication, and for supporting Soviet research stations in the Arctic Ocean and Antarctica. The Soviet Polar Aviation workhorse, the early 1950s-vintage piston-engined IL-14, had rendered sterling service for decades but was long since out of production and obsolete, and the surviving examples were approaching the limit of their useful life. Their imminent withdrawal after several service life extensions would leave Polar Aviation with no aircraft at all.

When contemplating the An-72 as a possible replacement for the IL-14, Aeroflot was more interested in greater payload and longer range than in STOL capability. The customer demanded a range of 4,500 km (2,795 miles); however, this and the required long endurance necessitated an increase in fuel capacity, which entailed a significant redesign of the airframe. On the other hand, the military were also interested in a version of the An-72 featuring longer range and endurance/on-station loiter time to be used as a border patrol aircraft (this eventually materialised as the An-72P described earlier). Thus it was possible to use a common airframe, the military and commercial versions differing only in avionics, equipment and cargo cabin layout. This made things easier for the Khar'kov aircraft factory, which was already tooling up for An-72 production. Yet the civil version took quite some time to achieve production status.

On 26th January 1983 the Council of Ministers issued a directive ordering the Kiev Mechanical Plant (that is, the Antonov OKB) to develop a civil version of the An-72; in keeping with the aircraft's intended primary role the civil version was initially designated An-72A (*ark**tich**eskiy* – Arctic). At first nobody at the OKB doubted in the least that the objective would be completed quickly. True, the changes introduced to meet the new requirements were quite extensive; but then, to save time the An-72A prototype could be converted from one of the original An-72 *sans suffixe* prototypes belonging to the OKB. The machine picked for conversion was the second prototype, CCCP-19793 (c/n 003).

As recounted in Chapter 1, the conversion involved cutting up the wings in order to mate new outer wings with trailing-edge sweep and reduced leading-edge sweep to the existing structure (with appropriate changes to the high-lift devices and ailerons) and introducing a 1.4-m (4 ft 7$\frac{7}{64}$ in) forward fuselage stretch. The wing span increased from 25.83 m (84 ft 8$\frac{15}{16}$ in) to 31.89 m (104 ft 7½ in), the wing area from 89.6 m^2 (963.4 sq ft) to 98.78 m^2 (1,062.1 sq ft) and the aspect ratio from 7.4 to 11.2. The fuel capacity rose to 16,250 litres (3,575 Imp gal) and the fuel load from 11 tons (24,250 lb) to 13,200 kg (29,100 lb).

Above: For the initial Arctic tests CCCP-780334 had icing visualisation stripes applied to the starboard wing, starboard air intake, fin and starboard tailplane.

The flightdeck was modified to feature a navigator's station aft of the captain's seat, and a hydrologist's workstation was provided on the port side aft of the entry door. Both workstations featured small observation blisters with teardrop fairings. A special dumping mechanism was installed at the cargo hatch sill for dropping items of cargo during parachute or free-fall delivery. The An-72A's maximum payload was 10 tons (22,045 lb).

Heated retractable skis equipped with scraper-type brakes were to be installed later on instead of the standard wheeled undercarriage. However, this required major structural modifications, and these plans eventually came to naught.

The work went ahead briskly at first. The An-72A prototype was completed in the late summer of 1983, receiving appropriate nose titles and the non-standard registration CCCP-780334. By then, however, the definitive designation An-74 already existed and was duly reflected in the registration.

It should be noted here that the highly unusual six-digit registrations encountered on some Antonov prototypes are explained as follows. The first and the last digits correspond to the aircraft type: 7****4 = An-74. By comparison, the two new-build An-32 prototypes (c/ns 001 and 003) of 1982 were initially registered CCCP-380122 and CCCP-380322; similarly, the An-71 prototypes of 1985-86 were CCCP-780151 and CCCP-780361. (However, this does not work with all Antonov types; cf. An-124 prototypes CCCP-680125, CCCP-680345 and An-225 CCCP-480182!) The meaning of the second digit, which is always an 8, remains unknown; this may be a code for the OKB's experimental shop. The

After the initial Arctic tests the An-74 prototype was refitted with a new radar in a longer 'droopsnoot' radome and reregistered CCCP-72003. It is seen here with the Le Bourget '87 exhibit code 324. The icing visualisation markings have been removed prior to the show.

CCCP-72003 comes in to land after a demonstration flight at Le Bourget. As you see, the Aeroflot titles on this aircraft were not only smaller than usual but red instead of black. Note also the red anti-collision lights, a leftover from An-72 CCCP-19793; the production An-72 had white ACLs as standard.

next two are the last two digits of the c/n (which is why CCCP-780334, the first An-74, has '03' – it refers to the An-72 airframe c/n 003 from which it was converted!). Finally, the last-but-one digit shows the year of manufacture; in this case, 3 = 1983.

(Speaking of which, the registrations of the An-72R prototypes (CCCP-783061, CCCP-783573 and CCCP-784072) do not really fit this pattern. The third and fourth digits are the last two of the c/n all right (365.720.10.930, 365.720.10.935 and 365.720.10.940), but the first and last digits add up to *different codes for each aircraft*, and in the case of CCCP-783061 we get An-71, which is not true! In the case of CCCP-783573 we get 73, which may explain the An-73 designation found in Western sources.)

As originally completed, CCCP-780334 retained the short and rather blunt radome characteristic of the An-72 prototypes. In keeping with its intended mission the aircraft wore Aeroflot's stylish polar colour scheme with red outer wings and horizontal tail (for high definition against white backgrounds in the event of a forced landing), a red/white vertical tail, a red cheatline and black Aeroflot titles. Actually the livery deviated a little from the standard: instead of being red with a broad horizontal white band, the vertical tail was divided into red (lower) and white (upper) halves and the Aeroflot titles were red. The colour division line on the wings coincided with the production break between the inner/outer wings.

On 29th September 1983 the An-72A made its maiden flight from Kiev-Svyatoshino to Kiev-Gostomel' at the hands of OKB test pilots Sergey A. Gorbik and V. A. Shlyakhov. This is where the programme, as one observer aptly put it, started plodding through treacle as an exceptionally lengthy test cycle began.

It became immediately apparent that the new wings had lost some of their stiffness (a natural result of the higher aspect ratio), which inevitably affected the aircraft's handling. The wing aerodynamics were also different (not least because of the cranked leading and trailing edges generating unwanted vortices), which reduced the efficiency of the high-lift devices to some extent. The An-72A was substantially heavier than the original short-fuselage/short-wing version; at the same time the larger wings generated more lift and turned the aircraft into a more avid flyer, somewhat limiting the ability to land on extremely short airstrips.

Still, the An-72A was well suited for cargo/passenger carriage and operations from ill-equipped airfields (or temporary airstrips) in the High North. Its long range and endurance rendered it suitable for such tasks as ice reconnaissance along the routes to be followed by ship convoys, supply flights to remote Polar bases and drifting research stations set up on ice floes in the Arctic Ocean.

The official designation An-72A existed until early 1985; then, as preparations for series production got under way, the aircraft was redesignated An-74 (largely in order to differentiate it from the military An-72) and the prototype's nose titles were altered accordingly. In the paperwork both variants were still designated *izdeliye* 72, although the first manufacturing drawings of the An-74 delivered to KhAPO in June 1984 featured a slightly different code (*izdeliye* 72.07). All subsequent civil versions were likewise designated An-74.

Arctic tests of the An-74 prototype began in April 1985. Operating from Amderma in the European part of Russia (on the Kara Sea coast) and Anadyr' on the coast of Chukotka in the Far East, CCCP-780334 made several flights to the archipelagos of Novaya Zemlya (New Land) and Zemlya Frantsa-Iosifa (Franz Joseph Land), Dixon Island, Mys Kamennyy (Stone Cape) and Bookhta Provideniya (Providence Bight). The missions also included ice reconnaissance in the Kara Sea and Anadyr' Bay. At this stage the leading edges of the fin, starboard wing, starboard stabiliser and starboard engine air intake had black zebra stripes applied for icing visualisation; the aircraft still had the original short radome.

In August 1985 the prototype underwent 'hot-and-high' performance testing in Tajikistan and Turkmenia. In January-March 1986 a new round of cold-weather tests was undertaken in Yakutia and the Arctic Ocean jointly with the State Civil Aviation Research Institute (GosNII GA – *Gosoo**dar**stvennyy na**ooch**no-is**sled**ovatel'skiy insti**toot** grazh**dahn**skoy avi-**ah**tsii*) as part of the manufacturer's flight test programme. This stage involved a rescue operation during which CCCP-780334 made two flights to the SP-27 drifting research station on 14th and 15th March (see Chapter 4 for more details of this mission).

The Arctic tests revealed that the flight-deck heating and windshield demisting were inadequate. The communications suite was worse; the VHF radio permitted radio contact with the SP-27 at no more than 400 km (250 miles) with the aircraft cruising at 11,000 m (36,090 ft), whereas the ground radio station at Chokurdakh, which was 1,650 km (1,025 miles) away, could communicate with the SP-27 without any trouble. The *Gradi**yent*** (Gradient) weather/navigation radar also proved to be a lemon and was later replaced by a different model.

Meanwhile, KhAPO was already manufacturing the first pre-production An-74 (c/n 365.720.10.947, f/n 0202) which received the 'MAP-style' registration CCCP-58642. (The 5864x series was one more of the 'mixed bag' registration blocks allocated to MAP aircraft and reused time and again. Earlier, the registration CCCP-58642 had been worn by Lisunov Li-2 c/n 6107 (in 1967-74) and Mil' Mi-4 c/n 06180 (in 1975-79), both of which belonged to the Antonov OKB.)

An-74 CCCP-58642 No.3 made its maiden flight on 26th June 1986. Outwardly it differed from the prototype only in having a more elongated radome (as fitted to the production-standard An-72) and a vertical tail painted in full conformity with the 'Polar' standard. In early August 1986 this aircraft made the An-74's international debut at an airshow in Vancouver, Canada. The initial registration

An-74s on the assembly line at the Khar'kov State Aircraft Manufacturing Co. The foremost aircraft appears to have been painted right in the final assembly shop (rather than making the first flight in natural metal form and going to the paint shop afterwards, as per normal practice) and the paint job is still incomplete.

Above and below: CCCP-58642, the pre-production An-74, had an An-72 style c/n (365.720.10.947; f/n 0202) and a production-standard elongated (but not drooped) radome. The difference in the tail colours and the style of the Aeroflot titles is obvious. Like the prototype, this aircraft still had a small rear observation blister.

proved to be short-lived; in 1989 it passed to an ex-Peruvian An-26 (c/n 5803), while the pre-production An-74 apparently became CCCP-74028.

Meanwhile, however, the prototype was undergoing modifications in order to cure the problems revealed by the Arctic experience. The most obvious change was the installation of a new radar in a new and longer radome; this differed in shape from the radome fitted to production An-72s, being bulged at the bottom and painted dark grey, which promptly earned it the nickname 'pelican nose'. A new TA-12 APU was also installed. It was in this guise that the prototype appeared at the 37th Paris Air Show in June 1987, wearing the new registration CCCP-72003 and the exhibit code 342. Apparently, however, the ungainly 'pelican nose' did not live up to the expectations and the production An-74 reverted to the more streamlined version already standardised on its military counterpart.

More action came in November 1987 when the An-74 prototype flown by an Antonov OKB crew delivered a stationary radio transceiver to Sredniy (= Middle) Island in the Kara Sea. In February-April 1988 the same aircraft flew a number of sorties in support of a Soviet-Canadian ski expedition following a 1,800-km (1,118-mile) route from Novaya Zemlya to Cape Columbia, N.W.T., across the North Pole. A mystery is associated with this expedition. Several photos exist of an An-74 (identifiable as the modified prototype by the 'pelican nose', the paint job on the vertical tail and the small red Aeroflot titles) carrying the expedition's emblem aft of the flightdeck and registered CCCP-72200. However, An-74 CCCP-72200 was never on the Soviet civil aviation register; moreover, CCCP-72003 has been seen many times *after* that and was last reported withdrawn from use at Kiev-Gostomel' in 2002! The above-mentioned photos are apparently *not* fakes with a retouched registration; makes you wonder what was the point of reregistering the aircraft for so brief a period before reverting to the old registration.

On 6th May 1988 the prototype set a world long-distance record in its class, covering 6,341.973 km (3,939 miles) non-stop from Moscow to Sovetskaya Gavan' ('Soviet Haven', a seaport in the Soviet Far East) on an orthodromic course. The aircraft was fitted with a long-range fuel tank for the occasion; but then, it was standard operational procedure for Polar Aviation IL-14s to carry such tanks.

On 2nd November 1988 An-74 CCCP-72003 departed Kiev-Gostomel', bound for Antarctica. The 17,000-km (10,560-mile) route took it across Italy, Cape Verde Islands, Brazil and Argentina to the Soviet Antarctic research stations of Bellingshausen, Novolazarevskaya and Molodyozhnaya. The culmination of the journey came when the crew captained by Antonov OKB test pilot V. Lysenko brought the first Antarctic inspection group headed by Artur N. Chilingarov, Vice-Chairman of the Soviet Union's State Committee for Hydrological and Weather Research (Goskomghidromet), to the Soviet research station Vostok located 3,488 m (11,443 ft) above sea level. Thus the An-74 made a tour of almost the entire glacial continent and became the first aircraft with a wheeled undercarriage to land on, and take off from, the so-called Pole of Cold near Ice Station Vostok – the coldest place on Earth where the ambient temperature reaches –83°C (–117°F).

A month later, on 29th December, the aircraft made an ambulance flight to Argentina from Ice Station Novolazarevskaya when a polar researcher was taken ill and required hospitalisation. A couple of days later CCCP-72003 was homeward bound with refuelling stops in Maputo, Aden and Larnaca, returning to Kiev on 6th January 1989. Thus, in the course of the Arctic and Antarctic compatibility trials the An-74 prototype covered a distance of more than 100,000 km (62,110 miles) in 65 flights!

Meanwhile, KhAPO was already turning out production An-74s – initially at a very low rate, both because the aircraft was not certified yet and because the military An-72 enjoyed higher priority. Curiously, the registrations assisted in telling the 'twins' from each other: the quasi-civil An-72s were registered in the CCCP-729xx block, while the An-74s received registrations in the CCCP-740xx series. The c/n was another giveaway – the second group of digits was 470 instead of 720 (except on the pre-production example), though logically it should have been 740.

The first production An-74, CCCP-74010 (c/n 365.470.30.450, f/n 0404) was released by the factory on 24th February 1987. It differed outwardly from the pre-production aircraft in having a greatly enlarged observation blister with no rear fairing at the hydrologist's station aft of the entry door. These two aircraft and four more production examples with large rear blisters – CCCP-74000 (c/n 365.470.60.649, f/n 0609), CCCP-74001 (c/n 365.470.70.655, f/n 0701), CCCP-74002 (c/n 365.470.70.682, f/n 0703) and CCCP-74003 (c/n 365.470.70.690, f/n 0705) – participated in the certification trials held jointly by MAP and MGA (specifically, the Antonov OKB and GosNII GA).

Here lies another puzzle. Some sources report that *four* pre-production (*sic*) An-74s commenced certification trials in January 1989. In May 1989 the trials had to be suspended due to an unspecified major problem and all four aircraft returned to Khar'kov for modifications and an additional series of manufacturer's flight tests. While these were in progress, a single An-74 (identity unknown) made a relief flight from Leningrad to Leninakan, participating in the effort to aid the victims of the disastrous earthquake which hit Armenia on 7th December 1988, destroying the cities of Kirovakan and Spitak, with a death toll of 25,000. The aircraft brought polar clothing and equipment which were urgently needed for rescuing people facing death from exposure in the mountains.

The problem is that, while CCCP-74002 was manufactured on 3rd January 1989 – that is, in time for the trials commencement date stated above, – CCCP-74000 is confirmed as (and CCCP-74001/CCCP-74003 reported as) manufactured on 31st August 1990. Theoretically this makes the participation of four An-74s in the trials as of January 1989 impossible. In reality, however, it is not unknown for aircraft to be officially manufactured several months and even years after they were first flown. Thus, 31st August 1990 may be the manufacture date *after all changes had been incorporated and tested*.

Anyway, once the problem had been cured, the certification trials resumed on 29th January 1990. After their completion, in accordance with the Soviet State Aircraft Register's directive No.14, on 2nd August 1991 the An-74 received Type Certificate No.13-74 stating its conformity to the YeNLGS-2 unified airworthiness regulations for fixed-wing aircraft (*Ye**din**yye **nor**my **lyot**noy **god**nosti samo**lyo**tov*). Under the certification trials programme alone, 47 test rigs had been built and the six aircraft involved had logged 7,104 flight hours in 5,109 test flights!

Like its military progenitor, the An-74 has several world records to its credit. In the spring of 1987 an OKB test crew captained by V. A. Tkachenko set five Class C-1 records in the 35... 45-ton (77,160... 99,200-lb) TOW category in a single flight, lifting a 15-ton (33,070-lb) payload to an altitude of 10,960 m (35,960 ft). Two months later, captained by the same pilot, the An-74 attained a maximum sustained altitude of 11,210 m (36,780 ft). As mentioned earlier, in May 1988 a crew captained by Yuriy N. Kotov set a long-distance record, covering a distance of 6,341.973 km in a straight line.

While the certification trials were still in progress, MAP decided to expand the future An-74 production by opening a second production line in Russia. In January 1991 it was decided to task the 'Polyot' (Flight) Omsk Aircraft Production Association (OAPO – ***Om**skoye aviatsi**on**noye proiz**vod**stvennoye obyedi**nen**iye 'Po**lyot**'*, ex-MAP aircraft factory No.166), with building the An-74. In the 1960s this plant had been transferred to the Ministry of General Machinery (MOM – *Mini**ster**stvo **ob**schchevo ma**shin**ostro**yen**iya*) responsible

Above and below: Seen here in 1990, the pre-production An-74 is resplendent in its Polar colours. Note the Doppler sensor panel offset to starboard under the main gear fairing and the way that the registration is carried well inboard on the wings (in black on grey, rather than in white on red as was customary).

Above: The first Omsk-built An-74 (RA-74050, c/n 47181011) kicks up a local snowstorm as it takes off on its maiden flight on 25th December 1993. The aircraft features a small observation blister at the navigator's station and a large observation blister aft of the entry door.

for the Soviet space and missile programmes; now MAP was trying to 'win back its own ground'. This was understandable, since the An-74 was envisaged as a successor to the obsolescent An-12 and An-26 turboprops; Aeroflot had quite a large fleet of both types, and one production line in Khar'kov might not be enough to ensure fleet renewal.

In 1991 two initial-production An-74s flew their final Polar mission, evacuating the personnel of Ice Station SP-30 which was disintegrating. Soon, however, the aircraft's fortunes suffered a dramatic change. First, the fourth production An-74 (CCCP-74002) crashed in Lensk, Yakutia, on 16th September 1991. Even though the crash was due to a combination of overload and pilot error, it certainly did not improve the aircraft's image. Then the Soviet Union ceased to exist, and so did the Soviet Polar research programme; the An-74 found itself 'laid off' – at any rate, as a Polar Aviation aircraft.

Nevertheless, KhAPO – now called Khar'kov State Aircraft Manufacturing Co. – continued producing the An-74 in the now-sovereign Ukraine in the hope of finding airline and/or industrial customers. As orders for the An-72 from the cash-strapped military dried up, the civil counterpart became the plant's only product for a while.

Meanwhile, in Russia not only OAPO but also the 'Progress' Aircraft Production Association named after N. I. Sazykin in the Far Eastern city of Arsen'yev (AAPO – *A**rsen'**yevskoye aviatsi**on**noye proiz**vod**stvennoye obyedi**nen**iye 'Pro**gress**'*, ex-MAP aircraft factory No.116) started gearing up for An-74 production in February 1993. AAPO was soon reoriented towards other programmes, notably the Kamov Ka-50 Black Shark attack helicopter, but OAPO persisted. In Omsk the An-74 received a new product code, *izdeliye* 47.000.

A shipset of airframe parts and systems components (c/n 365.470.98.94…, f/n 1704) was obtained from Khar'kov, and the pattern aircraft was duly assembled, receiving the new c/n 47181011 and the new f/n 0101P (the meaning of the P suffix is unknown). Registered RA-74050, the aircraft made its first flight on 25th December 1993 and was presented to invited guests and the press three days later; it was released by the factory on 21st April the following year.

Still, even the initial plans to build ten An-74s (for starters, that is) proved too optimistic. The 17th August 1998 Russian bank crisis forced many airlines to reconsider their purchase plans, and OAPO had to close down the An-74 production line after building no more than five examples, all from Ukrainian parts.

In Khar'kov, too, An-74 sales got off to a slow start, forcing the Antonov ANTK and the factory to start work on new versions of the twinjet tailored to customer demands. Back in 1992 the Ukrainian government had approved a national aircraft industry development programme; the An-74 figured strongly in it as the most sellable export product. The programme envisaged bolstering the aircraft's competitive potential and expanding its range of missions by developing a whole family of versions. Special importance was attached to extending the service life of the airframe and engines, increasing their time between overhauls and establishing a regional servicing and support network which was to ensure trouble-free operation worldwide.

No sooner said than done. The Antonov ANTK and the Khar'kov State Aircraft Manufacturing Co. developed new cargo, convertible and executive variants. A whole series of specialised variants optimised for ice reconnaissance by means of radar and laser systems, photo and video mapping, radar survey/mapping, cloud seeding in order to provoke rainfall and protect crops and the like against hail, weather research and so on was also proposed. Some of the versions are described below.

An-74MP light commercial transport

The An-74MP was the new baseline version featuring a substantially expanded avionics and equipment suite; this enabled it to fly

The test crew and invited guests pose beside An-74 RA-74050 after the first flight on 25th December 1993. Antonov ANTK General Designer Pyotr V. Balabuyev is seventh from left in the rear row.

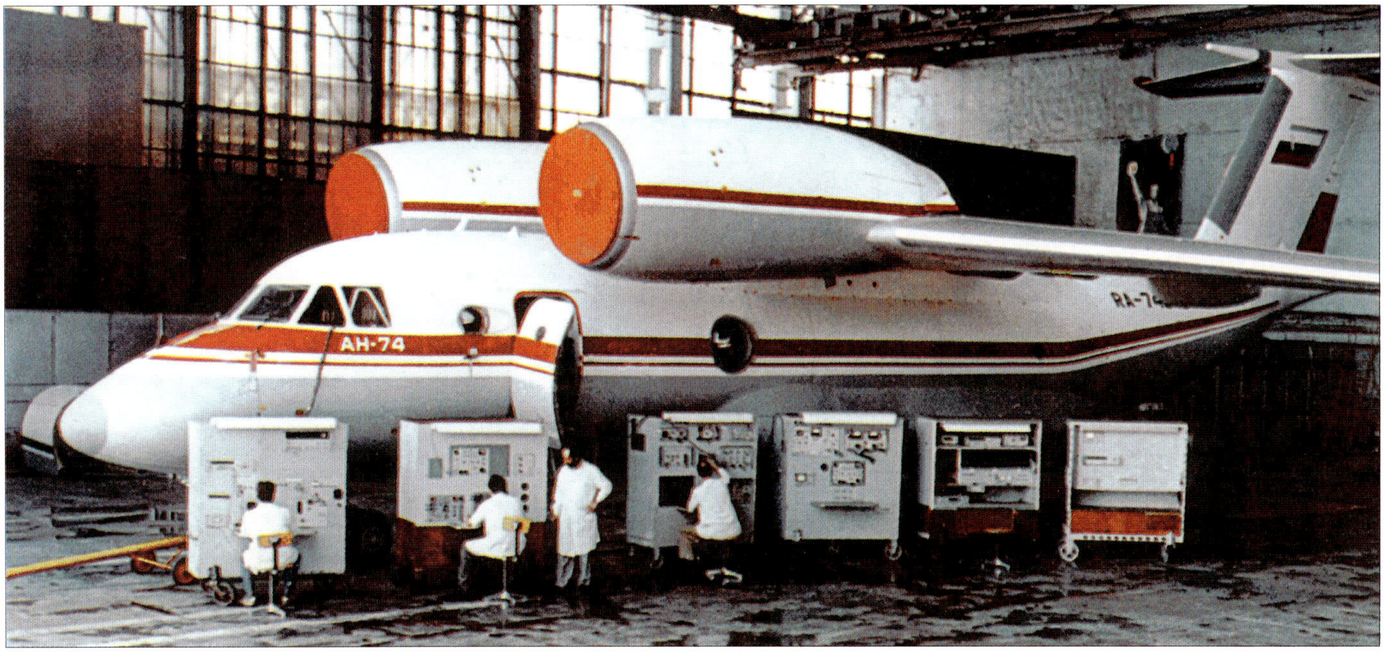

Above: An An-74 in non-standard Polar colours destined for a Russian customer (probably Shonkar or RDS-Avia) undergoes pre-delivery systems checks at the Khar'kov State Aircraft Manufacturing Co.

international cargo and, if necessary, passenger services without any limitations, hence the MP suffix standing for *mezhduna**rod**nyye po**lyo**ty* – international flights. The aircraft was tested and received a supplementary type certificate, becoming the basis for all subsequent versions.

An-74T (An-72AT) light commercial transport

Known as the An-72AT at the design stage, the An-74T (***trahns**portnyy* – [civil] transport, used attributively) was designed for a maximum payload of 10 tons (22,045 lb) as a 'pure' (that is, 'non-Polar') medium-haul freighter. The freight hold was equipped with a travelling overhead hoist and floor-mounted roller conveyors for container/pallet handling. Outwardly the An-74T differed from the original version in lacking the observation blisters.

The An-74T prototype was converted from the first production An-74, CCCP-74010; the navigator's blister was replaced by a simple window and the larger rear blister was substituted with a circular plug incorporating a regular-size window. Wearing the exhibit code 353, the aircraft made its debut at the 39th Paris Air Show in 1991 in blue/white Aeroflot colours. The same machine was displayed at the MAKS-93 airshow in Zhukovskiy (31st August/5th September 1993) wearing the Ukrainian registration UR-74010 and large 'ANTONOV 74T' titles.

In production form the aircraft had two sub-variants, the An-74T-100 and An-74T-200 (see below).

The An-74T prototype, CCCP-74010 (c/n 365.470.30.450, f/n 0404) at the 1991 Paris Air Show in company with a Yak-42 and the first prototype IL-114 (CCCP-54000). The absence of the observation blisters is obvious. Note the extended hydraulic supports under the rear fuselage.

Above: The same aircraft after conversion to a VIP aircraft for the Antonov ANTK's flying division, Antonov Airlines, seen here at Kiev-Svyatoshino during the second Aviasvit-XXI airshow (15th-18th September 2002). Note the large additional emergency exit to starboard and the extra cabin windows.

An-74TK-100 convertible light transport/regional airliner

The need for a convertible variant of the An-74 was dictated by the presence of routes where an aircraft could be carrying cargo one way and picking up passengers on the return trip (or vice versa). Experience showed that a single aircraft with a quick-change interior was more viable economically in these conditions than using separate airliners and freighters.

Thus the An-74TK-100 (***trahns**portnyy, konver**teer**uyemyy*) is a convertible/combi version that can carry up to 8.5-10 tons (18,740-22,045 lb) of cargo or up to 52 passengers. In the latter case the passenger cabin is outfitted with four-abreast seats with a central aisle, enclosed overhead luggage bins, a galley, a public address system and an oxygen system. The overhead luggage bins incorporate passenger service units with individual ventilation nozzles, reading lights and flight attendant call buttons.

Access to the cabin is via the cargo ramp which is partially lowered and equipped with boarding steps and handrails, or via the entry door which features a fold-away boarding ladder with a handrail akin to that of the An-24. Stepped lightweight racks for carry-on baggage are suspended from the cabin ceiling above the cargo ramp; the baggage compartment is separated from the cabin by a lightweight bulkhead.

Safety requirements applicable to the airliner configuration necessitated structural changes making the An-74TK-100 easy to identify. The usual ICAO Type III emergency

Another view of UR-74010 in its current guise at Kiev-Svyatoshino, showing the airstair door.

Above: Seen here on final approach to Moscow-Domodedovo, RA-74001 (c/n 365.470.70.655, f/n 0701) operated by the now-defunct Sakha Avia was probably the first example converted to An-74T-100 standard. The extra emergency exit is obvious but the extra windows are somewhat harder to see.

exit measuring 0.51 x 0.915 m (1 ft 8$\frac{5}{64}$ in x 3 ft 0$\frac{1}{32}$ in) on the starboard side of the rear fuselage is augmented by an identical exit on the opposite side plus a Type I emergency exit measuring 0.61 x 1.22 m (2 ft 0$\frac{1}{64}$ in x 4 ft 0$\frac{1}{32}$ in) on the starboard side of the forward fuselage. Additional windows are also provided to admit daylight into the cabin; the window arrangement is door+2 windows+1+exit+1 to port and exit+1+1+exit+1 to starboard.

Alternatively, in a combi layout the aircraft can carry 12 passengers plus 6 tons (13,230 lb) of cargo, or 20 passengers plus 4.5 tons (9,920 lb) of cargo. In these cases the aircraft carries a movable bulkhead separating the passenger cabin at the front from the cargo compartment in the back; it is stowed on the port side of the baggage compartment to permit loading and unloading. Working together with restraining nets, this bulkhead is stressed to withstand a longitudinal load of 9 Gs in a crash landing, protecting the passengers from being crushed by the cargo.

The crew of four (captain, first officer, navigator and flight engineer) can transform the aircraft from 52-seat configuration to a pure freighter within three hours or so. It works like this: first, the seat backs are folded forward and the double seat units tip up to lie flat against the cabin walls. Then the carpeted

UR-74038, the Khar'kov factory's An-74TK-200 demonstrator (c/n 365.470.97.933, f/n 1605) takes off from Farnborough's runway 25 at the Farnborough International 2004 airshow. Again, the extra windows and port side emergency exit are very much in evidence. The type is painted on simply as 'An-74TK'.

Two views of the same aircraft as unveiled at the MAKS-95 airshow in Zhukovskiy. The aircraft wore correct 'An-74TK-200' nose titles then. Note the lack of a window ahead of the entry door revealing the absence of a navigator's station and indicating that the aircraft has a crew of two.

Above: Gazpromavia An-74T-100 RA-74008 (c/n 365.470.95.900, f/n 1403) basks in the sun at its home base of Moscow-Ostaf'yevo, showing the navigator's station window. As the stickers on the fuselage indicate, it was chartered as a TV crew support aircraft during the 2002 Paris-Dakar rally.

Above: Gazpromavia's An-74TK-100S ambulance aircraft, RA-74005, offloads a patient with a GAZ-27051 GAZelle ambulance waiting. '03' is the ambulance phone number in Russia. Note the airstair door.

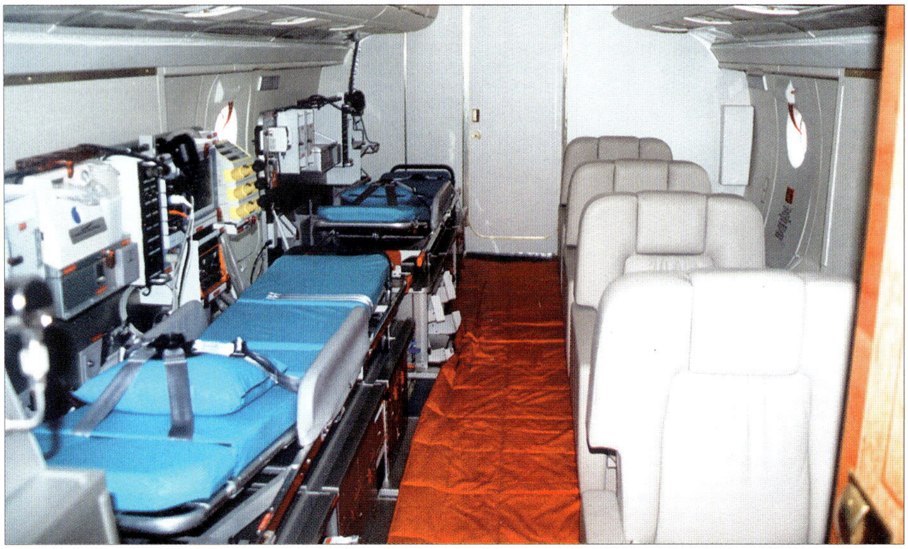

The rear cabin of RA-74005, showing the two stretchers and medical equipment to starboard and four seats for the medical attendants to port.

false floor panels fold up as well and are secured to the walls, enclosing the seat units to protect them against damage by the cargo. Next, the overhead luggage bins are collapsed and secured to the walls; the cabin's rear bulkhead and carry-on baggage racks are dismantled and stowed. Now the cargo tie-down fittings and optional roller tracks on the cabin floor are exposed and the aircraft is ready for loading.

The cargo handling equipment includes an overhead hoist. On routes with stable cargo traffic the aircraft can be fitted with equipment for loading and securing LD-3 or LD-6 containers and 2L3P or LD-3 pallets.

The data placard in front of An-74 RA-74025 displayed at the MAKS-93 airshow in Aviacor colours misidentified it as an An-74TK-100; in fact it was a standard An-74 with two observation blisters of unequal size. The first true An-74TK-100 was probably RA-74001 converted from a 'straight' An-74 for Sakha Avia. The CIS Interstate Aviation Committee's Aircraft Register granted a type certificate for the An-74TK-100 on 4th August 1995.

An-74TK-100S convertible light transport/ambulance aircraft

A single An-74 owned by Gazpromavia (RA-74005, c/n 365.470.94.892, f/n 1310) was outfitted for ambulance duties in the process of conversion to An-74TK-100 standard. Its primary role is the transportation of injured or critically ill personnel from oilfields to Moscow where qualified medical services are available. Designated An-74TK-100S (*sani**tar**nyy* – medical), the aircraft has a cabin divided into two sections. The forward section is a VIP cabin with club-four seating and tables; the rear section is the sick bay featuring two stretchers to starboard (in tandem) and four seats for medical attendants to port. Medical equipment enabling life support en route is mounted on the starboard wall.

The An-74TK-100S was demonstrated statically at the Civil Aviation-2002 airshow held at Moscow-Domodedovo from 14th to 18th August 2002.

An-74TK-200 convertible light transport/regional airliner

A convertible/combi version similar to the An-74TK-100 but with a flightdeck configured for a crew of two is designated An-74TK-200. Outwardly it differs from the An-74TK-100 only in lacking the navigator's station window to port aft of the flightdeck windows. The aircraft can be operated on routes where ground services are provided.

The An-74TK-200 prototype, UR-74038 (c/n 365.470.97.933, f/n 1605) was demonstrated for the first time at the MAKS-95 airshow (22nd-27th August 1995) in a basically

Above: The as-yet unpainted An-74T-200 prototype (c/n 365.470.99.1021, f/n 2004) drops an item of cargo during pre-delivery tests, using the parachute extraction method. The position of the cargo ramp slid forward under the fuselage is clearly visible, as are the different shades of metal skin and GRP/CFRP panels giving the aircraft a patchwork appearance. Unusually, the aircraft carries no test registration.

Right: An appropriately marked An-74T-200 in three-tone camouflage colours awaiting delivery to the Iranian Revolutionary Guard at Khar'kov-Sokol'nikovo. Note that the door is outlined in yellow.

Below: Another view of the same aircraft taxying during pre-delivery tests. So far Iran is the only military operator of the An-74, though Egypt has ordered the An-74T-200A as well and Libya is next in line.

Above: Bearing appropriate nose titles, anonymous-looking An-74D RA-74048 (c/n 365.470.98.943, f/n 1701) operated by the 2nd Sverdlovsk Air Enterprise is seen here at Kiev-Svyatoshino during the 2002 Aviasvit-XXI airshow. Note the extra windows, the airstair door and the blade aerial ahead of the fin serving additional communications equipment.

white colour scheme with correct nose titles. Two years later, the same aircraft appeared at the MAKS-97 (19th-24th August 1997) in a new Khar'kov State Aircraft Manufacturing Co. demonstration livery but with 'An-74TK' nose titles; it has been a regular performer at various airshows ever since.

An-74TK-200S convertible light transport/ambulance aircraft

This designation applies to an ambulance version of the An-74TK-200 similar to the An-74TK-100S which is now offered by the Khar'kov State Aircraft Manufacturing Co.

An-74T-100 light commercial transport

The An-74T-100 is a non-convertible version of the An-74T with a crew of four optimised for operation in areas with inadequate navigation aids. The cargo handling equipment permits loading and unloading of single items weighing up to 2.5 tons (5,510 lb). The maximum take-off weight is 36.5 tons (80,470 lb) and the maximum payload is 10 tons.

An-74T-200 light commercial/ military transport

This, again, is a non-convertible version of the An-74T but with a two-man flightdeck. The aircraft can transport up to 10 tons of cargo, including up to 1,000 kg (2,200 lb) secured to the ramp, at 550-700 km/h (341-434 mph) to a distance of up to 1,350 km (838 miles); maximum range with a 3.5-ton (7,720-lb) payload is 4,000 km (2,484 miles). The An-74T-200 can operate from concrete, gravel or dirt/grass runways.

The prototype (c/n 365.470.99.1021, f/n 2004) was delivered to Iran as 15-2250.

An-74-200 light commercial transport/passenger aircraft

The An-74-200 differs from the baseline An-74 primarily in being powered by D-36 Srs 3A engines instead of Srs 1As or Srs 2As, which allowed the maximum take-off weight to be increased to 36.5 tons. Range with a 7.5-ton (16,530-lb) payload is increased from 1,650 to 2,000 km (from 1,025 to 1,240 miles). The overwing engine placement screens the engine exhaust and reduces the noise footprint, allowing the aircraft to meet the requirements set by the modern Russian AP-36 airworthiness regulations (equivalent to the US FAR Pt 36).

The An-74-200 prototype, CCCP-74008 (c/n 365.470.95.900, f/n 1403), was manufactured on 29th April 1992. This aircraft owned by the Antonov ANTK and painted in basic Aeroflot polar colours was demonstrated statically and in flight at the MAKS-93, performing barrel rolls and half-loops.

An-74T-200A light commercial transport

This is a derivative of the An-74-200 lacking provisions for passenger carriage. The aircraft can transport up to 10 tons of cargo, including up to 1,000 kg secured to the ramp, at 600-700 km/h (372-434 mph) to a distance of up to 1,350 km; maximum range with a 3-ton (6,620-lb) payload is 4,200 km (2,608 miles). The An-74T-200 can operate systematically from unpaved runways.

An-74P-100 executive transport

This designation applies to an executive version of the An-74 with a VIP cabin, a rest area

A computer-generated image of the proposed all-cargo An-74T-300, showing the underslung D-436T1 engines. Curiously, the computer artists have put a Ukrainian flag on the tail. despite the Russian registration.

Above: The An-74TK-300 prototype, appropriately registered UR-74300 (c/n 365.470.98.984, f/n 1910) takes off on a demonstration flight from Zhukovskiy's runway 12 at the MAKS-2001 airshow, wearing the exhibit code 501. As this view shows, the An-74's main gear units can retract or extend independently.

Another view of the prototype, showing well the underwing engine placement, the separate core/bypass flow nozzles of the D-436T1 and the window arrangement. On the An-72/An-74 the landing gear retraction sequence begins with the main units.

with bunks and room for a vehicle in the back. The aircraft is equipped with a communications suite enabling continuous interaction with business centres on the ground, including a telephone and a fax machine; 'creature comforts' include a TV with a video player, a bar/drinks cooler and a galley. The maximum TOW is increased to 34.8 tons (76,720 lb), including a 10-ton payload.

Quite possibly this description applies to the two An-74s operated by the Russian Ministry for Civil Aid and Protection (EMERCOM of Russia) – RA-74029 (c/n 365.470.97.940, f/n 1609) and RA-74034 (c/n 47136012, f/n 0102P). These aircraft have been referred to in the press as An-74Ps, but – see this designation below.

An-74D (An-74-200) executive transport

Another executive version, the An-74D (alias An-74-200D; again, the suffix stands for *delo**voy*** – executive or business, used attributively), can transport 12 passengers in style. The cabins feature additional soundproofing and heat insulation, luxurious furnishings and upholstery, an audio/video in-flight entertainment system and so on. Satellite navigation equipment is available as an optional kit.

Two aircraft, RA-74012 (c/n 365.470.98.959, f/n 1710) and RA-74048 (c/n 365.470.98.943, f/n 1701), have been reported as An-74Ds, and the latter actually carries these nose titles. The former aircraft was in the static park at the MAKS-95 airshow, billed as an An-74-200 but already equipped with a VIP interior. RA-74048 differs in having a windowless airstair door replacing the normal forward-hinged door and boarding ladder. An-74T UR-74010 was possibly also redesignated An-74D following refit as an executive transport and repaint in full Antonov Airlines colours in 2001.

An-74BK executive transport

One more executive version was designated An-74BK (standing for ***biz**nes-**k**lass*). It is roughly equivalent to the An-72S, differing in avionics and equipment. There are three passenger cabins accommodating up to 16 passengers and room for a car or jeep in the back. The aircraft is equipped with a telephone, a fax machine, a bar and a galley.

According to press reports, the first An-74BK was ordered by the KamAZ automobile factory (***Kam**skiy avtomo**bil'**nyy za**vod***) in Naberezhnyye Chelny, Tatarstan, with delivery due for 1995. Interestingly, RA-74012 (listed above as an An-74D) has been seen with the KamAZ logo on the fuselage!

An-74VIP executive transport

This version proposed by the Khar'kov State Aircraft Manufacturing Co. is basically similar in concept to the versions described above, offering maximum comfort for 'Mr. Big' and his retinue plus room for bulky cargo or an automobile. The demands of the most exacting customers are to be met by subcontracting the interior outfitting job to the leading Western specialist companies, such as Diamonite Aircraft Furnishings. There were plans to equip the An-74VIP with an adequate number of large cabin windows (to avoid claustrophobia!), an airstair door and enhanced soundproofing features.

An-74TK-300 convertible light transport/regional airliner

The latest version of the An-74 to exist in hardware form is the substantially redesigned An-74TK-300 based on the An-74TK-200. It was developed as a joint effort by the Antonov ANTK, the Khar'kov State Aircraft Manufacturing Co., ZMKB Progress, the Motor-Sich engine plant and various systems subcontractors, with support from the CIS Interstate Aviation Committee, LII, GosNII GA and the Aeronavigatsiya (Air Navigation) Centre.

This aircraft relinquished the An-72/An-74's characteristic overwing engine placement, as a modern airliner in this category has no real use for upper-surface blowing and STOL performance. Instead of the two high-set D-36 Srs 3As the An-74TK-300 is powered by two 7,500-kgp (16,530-lbst) Muravchenko (ZMKB Progress) D-436T1 turbofans in underwing nacelles carried on pylons attached to the inner wing sections. The engines feature cascade-type thrust reversers on the bypass flow enclosed by translating cowls. The overall dimensions are identical to those of the An-74TK-200; so is the fuselage design, except for the forward airstair door and the number of cabin windows.

The D-436T1 is 20% more fuel-efficient than the D-36 powering the other aircraft of the family, with a specific fuel consumption of 264 g/tonne-km versus 340 g/tonne-km; this is expected to improve the aircraft's operating economy appreciably – an all-important factor for airlines, especially small carriers operating local services (such as might be expected to order the An-74TK-300). Also, the low-set pylon-mounted engines are more readily accessible, simplifying maintenance; as for FOD, this is not a major problem at more-or-less well-maintained airports where the runways are habitually swept clean.

The new engine placement has also improved the aircraft's aerodynamics to a certain extent, increasing the cruising speed from 700 to 750 km/h (from 434 to 465 mph). The aircraft can operate from runways 1,650 m (5,410 ft) long or longer. Possible interior configurations include an all-cargo layout, a version seating 52 passengers four-abreast at 75 cm (29½ in) pitch, or a combi layout.

The An-74TK-300 has a maximum range of 3,500 km (2,173 miles) in 52-seat configuration or 1,500 km (931 miles) in all-cargo configuration – a 50% increase as compared to the An-74TK-200. It fully meets current noise and pollution regulations and navigation accuracy requirements.

Another characteristic feature of the new version is the greatly increased number of cabin windows to provide adequate lighting. The window arrangement is door+7+exit+1 to port and exit+7+exit+1 to starboard (that is, nine windows to port and ten to starboard).

Contrary to normal practice, the prototype (c/n 365.470.98.984, f/n 1910) was built not at the Antonov ANTK's experimental plant in Kiev but at the production plant in Khar'kov by converting an as-yet unflown An-74TK-200 airframe. By then it was customary to allocate letter-only registrations to new Ukrainian aircraft, but the An-74TK-300 prototype received the custom registration UR-74300. Bearing the legend 'Ukraine' on the fuselage and the large numerals '300' on the tail, the aircraft made its maiden flight at Khar'kov-Sokol'nikovo on 20th April 2001, piloted by Antonov ANTK test pilot A. A. Kroots (captain), factory test pilot V. P. Samodoorov (co-pilot), factory flight engineer V. I. Zhookov and Antonov ANTK test engineer A. S. Makiyan.

Shortly afterwards the An-74TK-300 made its world debut at the 44th Paris Air Show, wearing a revised colour scheme similar to that of An-74TK-200 UR-74038 and the exhibit code 413. From 14th to 19th August 2001 the aircraft was displayed at the MAKS-2001 airshow in Zhukovskiy with a new exhibit code, 501, which was rather strange (Moscow airshows do not follow the practice of applying such codes).

The certification trials to AP-25 airworthiness regulations (equivalent to FAR Pt 25) included 219 flights and were to be completed in July 2002, with a type certificate expected in September. The Antonov ANTK and the plant launched a large-scale promotional campaign. Several orders have reportedly been secured from Russia and China; the first letter of intent was signed on 26th July 2002 at the Farnborough International airshow by Aeroflot Russian Airlines which intended to buy five aircraft in a 10-12-seat executive configuration (probably to be operated by the Aeroflot-Plus business charter subsidiary as a Tu-134AK replacement). The IFK-Jet (Il'yushin Finance Co.) leasing company also evinced an interest, planning to order more than 30 An-74TK-300s in airline and VIP versions.

Since 2003, however, no news has been forthcoming on any sales of the An-74TK-300. The only 'customer' was the Ukrainian government flight based at Kiev-Borispol' and known as the Ukraine Air Enterprise, which leased the prototype in 2003. Originally retaining its alphanumeric registration, it was later reregistered UR-LDK.

An-74T-300 light commercial transport (project)

This designation applies to a projected all-cargo version of the An-74TK-300.

An-74MP-300 patrol aircraft (project)

An armed derivative of the An-74TK-300 powered by 6,500-kgp D-36 Srs 4 engines is under development as a successor to the An-72P.

Above: An artist's impression of the An-74TK-300P airliner. The rear fuselage stretch is evident.

An-74TK-300P regional airliner

The Khar'kov State Aircraft Manufacturing Co. has proposed an all-passenger derivative of the An-74TK-300. The aircraft is to feature a rear fuselage stretch increasing the overall length to 30.82 m (101 ft $1\frac{3}{8}$ in) and the seating capacity to 66 or 70 passengers. The rear cargo door and ramp are eliminated; the window arrangement is door+13+door to port and exit+13+exit to starboard.

The aircraft is to be powered by D-36 Srs 4 engines. The maximum TOW is 37.5 tons (82,670 lb), including a 10-ton payload; cruising speed is 725 km/h (450 mph). The crew comprises two pilots and two flight attendants.

An-174 light commercial transport (project)

This aircraft looking like a stretched An-74TK-300 was developed in parallel as an An-12 replacement. This designation may have been changed to An-74TK-400 in the meantime (see next entry).

An-74TK-400 convertible light transport/regional airliner (project)

In 2000, mention was made in the press of a stretched version designated An-74TK-400. Little has been revealed, except that the maximum payload is 12 tons (26,455 lb).

An-74T-200V light military transport (project)

Development of An-72 versions for military customers ceased after the break-up of the Soviet Union due to lack of orders (explained by political and financial problems). However, the Antonov ANTK and the Khar'kov State Aircraft Manufacturing Co. have been working on military versions incorporating all the improvements introduced on the commercial An-74 in the meantime.

Designated An-74T-200V (*voy**e**nnyy* – military), a proposed follow-on to the An-72 is to carry materiel weighing up to 10 tons or 44 fully equipped troops and be capable of paradropping cargo or troopers.

An-74P border patrol aircraft (project)

The An-74T-200V evolved into a further military project – a border patrol aircraft similar to the An-72P. Designated An-74P (*patr**oo**l'nyy*), the machine is to be used for patrolling the state borders and economic exclusion zone, as well as for fulfilling the same transport missions as the An-74T-200V.

An-74 avionics testbed

At the closing stages of its flying career the An-74 prototype (CCCP-72003) was converted into an avionics testbed with a magnetic anomaly detector (MAD) boom with a dielectric bulge at the end (looking like a huge matchstick) projecting aft from the tailcone.

The An-74 prototype, CCCP-72003, ended its days as an avionics testbed equipped with an MAD boom projecting aft from the suitably cropped tailcone. The bulged dielectric tip fairing is missing here.

Above: With at least two An-12s in the background, CCCP-72003 is seen at Pushkin airfield near Leningrad where the conversion was probably done. The bulge at the end of the MAD boom is clearly visible here.

Another view of CCCP-72003 at Pushkin.

Chapter 3

A Closer Look

The following structural description applies to the basic production-standard An-72. Details of other versions are indicated as appropriate.

Type: Twin-engined STOL tactical military transport (An-72) and commercial transport (An-74). The airframe is basically of all-metal riveted and bonded construction utilising high-strength aluminium alloys and honeycomb structures. Some airframe components are made of composites (glassfibre reinforced plastic and carbonfibre reinforced plastic); their aggregate weight is 980 kg (2,160 lb), which gives an overall weight saving of 350 kg (771 lb).

The aircraft is designed for a service life of 40,000 hours and 20,000 cycles over a 20-year period. Time between overhauls is 6,000 hours, 6,000 cycles and seven years; the guaranteed time until the first overhaul is 9,000 hours, 9,000 cycles or ten years, whichever comes first.

Fuselage: Semi-monocoque stressed-skin structure of beam-and-stringer construction with frames. The fuselage cross-section is basically circular, changing to elliptical with the longer axis horizontal in the extreme nose (ahead of the flightdeck windshield) and in the rear fuselage. Maximum fuselage diameter is 3.1 m (10 ft 2$^{3}/_{64}$ in).

Structurally the fuselage is made up of four sections: the forward fuselage, the centre fuselage, the rear fuselage and the aft fuselage (tailcone). All sections are joined by flanges. The greater part of the fuselage is pressurised.

The *forward fuselage (Section F1)* includes the flightdeck, which is separated from the rest of the pressurised cabin by a rigid bulkhead with a pressure door, and the foremost portion of the freight hold. The foremost frame is the kinked forward pressure bulkhead mounting the weather radar dish; the GRP radome of honeycomb construction with ten lightning protection strips opens upwards and is secured by five Camloc tension locks. The nosewheel well is located immediately aft of the pressure bulkhead. It is flanked by two avionics bays below the flightdeck floor, with upward-opening CFRP access covers on both sides; each cover is held in place by six Dzus fasteners.

The An-72 has a crew of three; the 'straight' An-74 and An-74 Srs 100 are configured for a crew of four, with a navigator's station behind the captain's seat to port and a flight engineer's station behind the co-pilot's seat. The An-74 Srs 200 and An-74TK-300 have a two-man flightdeck. The flightdeck glazing features a one-piece frame with two curved windshield panels and two side windows on each side; hydraulically-powered windshield wipers are provided. On the short-fuselage prototypes the foremost pair of side

Above: The forward and centre fuselage of the An-72P prototype ('06 Yellow'). Note the starboard-side observation blister characteristic of this version and the nose-mounted landing lights (prototype only).

A view of the An-72P's nose, showing the radome with lightning protection strips, the sliding direct vision windows and the metal deflector ahead of the navigator's observation blister.

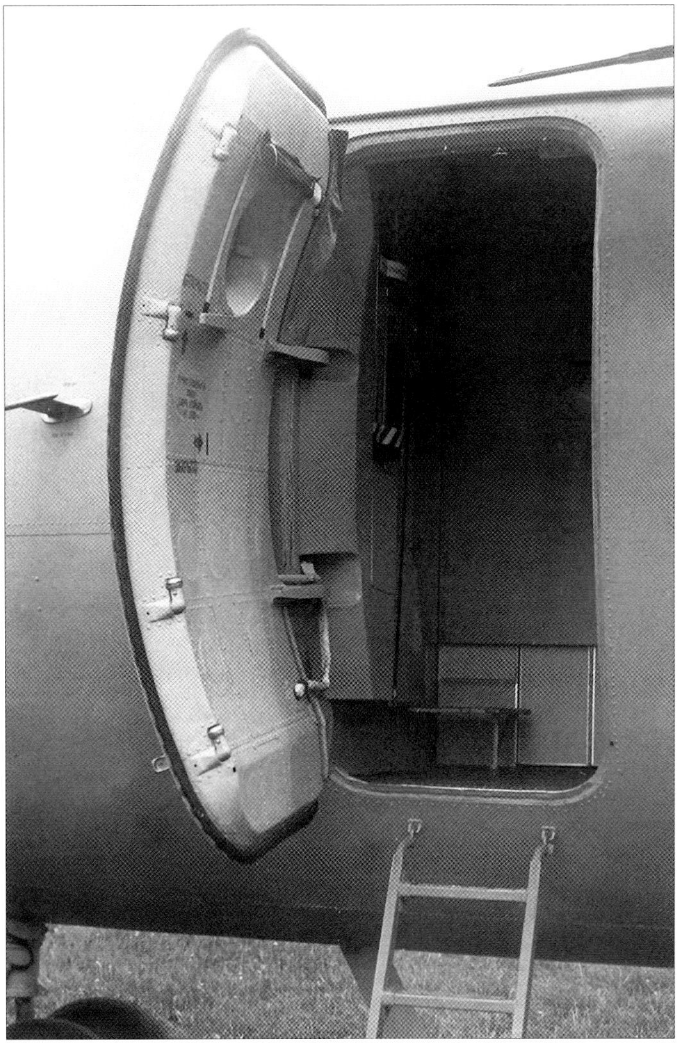

Above: The rear fuselage and tailcone of An-72 c/n 365.720.10.952 (f/n 0204). The one-piece CFRP rear cargo door is in the middle of its rearward travel. Note the rear triangular blade aerial of the *izdeliye* 62-01 (Parol') IFF transponder.

Left: The open entry door of An-72 c/n 365.720.10.952 reveals the hefty hinges, the low-set hydraulic ram for emergency actuation (for bailing out), the rolled-up curtain above the window and the step leading to the elevated flightdeck.

Below: The centre fuselage of the An-72P prototype, showing the forward portion of the GRP main landing gear fairing (incorporating a standard landing light) and the port forward cabin window.

Above right: A Polish-built Nysa 521 minibus (outfitted as a mobile laboratory by the Polish company Elwro) with the post-1981 number plate 3659 KhAA (indicating it is registered in Khar'kov) is driven up the ramp of an An-72.

Below left: A GAZ-24 Volga with the pre-1981 number plate 41-50 KKhR is apparently secured to the cargo ramp. However, the ramp obviously won't close in this position, as the rear pressure door will crush the car's rear end!

ELWRO
3659 XAA

Above: The overhead hoist in the cabin of the basic An-72 and An-74 runs on rails and has a lifting capacity of 2.5 tons (5,510 lb)

A look inside the freight hold of an An-72. Note the vehicle loading guide lines on the cargo ramp.

windows are sliding direct vision windows which can be used for emergency evacuation on the ground; only the port forward side window opens in this fashion on production aircraft. There is also an inward-opening square-shaped escape hatch measuring 0.5 x 0.5 m (1 ft 7 11/16 in x 1 ft 7 11/16 in) in the flightdeck roof providing access to the upper surface of the aircraft for maintenance purposes.

The windshield is made of birdproof triplex silicate glass and features electric de-icing; all other flightdeck windows have Perspex glazing. The An-72P and 'straight' An-74 have a transparent observation blister with a rear fairing on the port side at the navigator's station; on some An-74 variants it is replaced by a circular window to provide natural lighting for the navigator.

A rectangular forward-hinged entry door measuring 0.9 x 1.65 m (2 ft 11 7/16 in x 5 ft 4 31/32 in) with a small circular window is located on the port side at the rear of Section F1; the door opens outward through 90° and may be actuated hydraulically to act as a slipstream deflector for bailing out. This necessitates the use of a detachable boarding ladder; in contrast, the An-74D and An-74TK-300 have a downward-hinged windowless airstair door of identical dimensions obviating the need for a ladder.

The *centre fuselage (Section F2)* accommodates the freight hold which can be decompressed in flight for paradropping cargo or troops, leaving the flightdeck pressurised. The cargo hold measures 10.5 x 2.15 x 2.2 m (34 ft 5 25/64 in x 7 ft 0 21/32 in x 7 ft 2 5/8 in), with a volume of 54 m^3 (1,907 cu ft); the cargo door sill height of the unladen aircraft is 1.5 m (4 ft 11 in). The An-74TK-200 has a shorter (9.95 m/32 ft 7 3/4 in) but slightly wider (2.2 m) cabin.

Two fuselage mainframes serve as attachment points for the wing centre section's front and rear spars respectively. The wing/fuselage joint is enclosed by a fairing whose front and rear sections are made of GRP.

Two full-size windows are provided on each side at the front and rear of the freight hold; the rear starboard window is incorporated into a rectangular ICAO Type III emergency exit measuring 0.51 x 0.915 m (1 ft 8 5/64 in x 3 ft 0 1/32 in). The port forward window is replaced by a large hemispherical blister on some An-74s. The convertible variants (An-74TK-100/-200/-300) feature an identical Type III emergency exit located symmetrically to port, a larger (ICAO Type I) emergency exit measuring 0.61 x 1.22 m (2 ft 0 1/64 in x 4 ft 0 1/32 in) on the starboard side of the forward fuselage and six additional cabin windows (fore and aft of each emergency exit).

A large flat-bottomed GRP fairing is located on the centre fuselage underside. It accommodates the main landing gear units

Above: This view shows the load-bearing structure of the rear fuselage and more details of the hoist.

(the mainwheel wells are separated by the fuselage keel beam), the APU (in the rear section on the starboard side) and various equipment items. There are two underfloor equipment bays accessible via removable covers in the freight hold floor.

The upswept *rear fuselage (Section F3)* is cut away from below; the cutout is closed by a cargo ramp and a flat rear pressure bulkhead swinging upwards and aft. The roof of the rear fuselage incorporates a tail unit inspection window offset to starboard and an inward-opening escape hatch measuring 0.5 x 0.5 m on the centreline just ahead of the fin, used in the event of ditching.

The cargo ramp is actuated by twin hydraulic rams and can be opened in two ways, depending on the type of cargo handling operations in hand. In one position it hinges down conventionally to serve as a ramp for vehicle loading. Alternatively, the ramp can be lowered and slid forward under the centre fuselage to permit loading cargoes directly from a truck bed or paradropping troops, cargoes or vehicles. In so doing the front end of the ramp travels along a track on the fuselage centreline, while the rear end swings down on the partially extended hydraulic rams acting as linkages.

The unpressurised *aft fuselage (Section F4)* is mated to Section F3 along a sloping former and likewise cut away from below. Its aft extremity is horizontally flattened. The cutout is closed by a cargo door – a one-piece CFRP structure sliding aft on a centreline track (except on the first two An-72 prototypes which had outward-hinged clamshell doors). The cargo hatch aperture has a length of 7.1 m (23 ft 3$\frac{17}{32}$ in) and a maximum width of 2.4 m (7 ft 10½ in). The rear/aft fuselage carries the tail unit.

Wings: Cantilever shoulder-mounted monoplane wings of basically trapezoidal planform, mounted above the fuselage to avoid

There are tip-up seats along the freight hold walls, and a third row can be installed on the centreline in case of need. Note the detachable covers giving access to the underfloor equipment bay. Note the overhead lights and the cable along the starboard wall powering the overhead hoist.

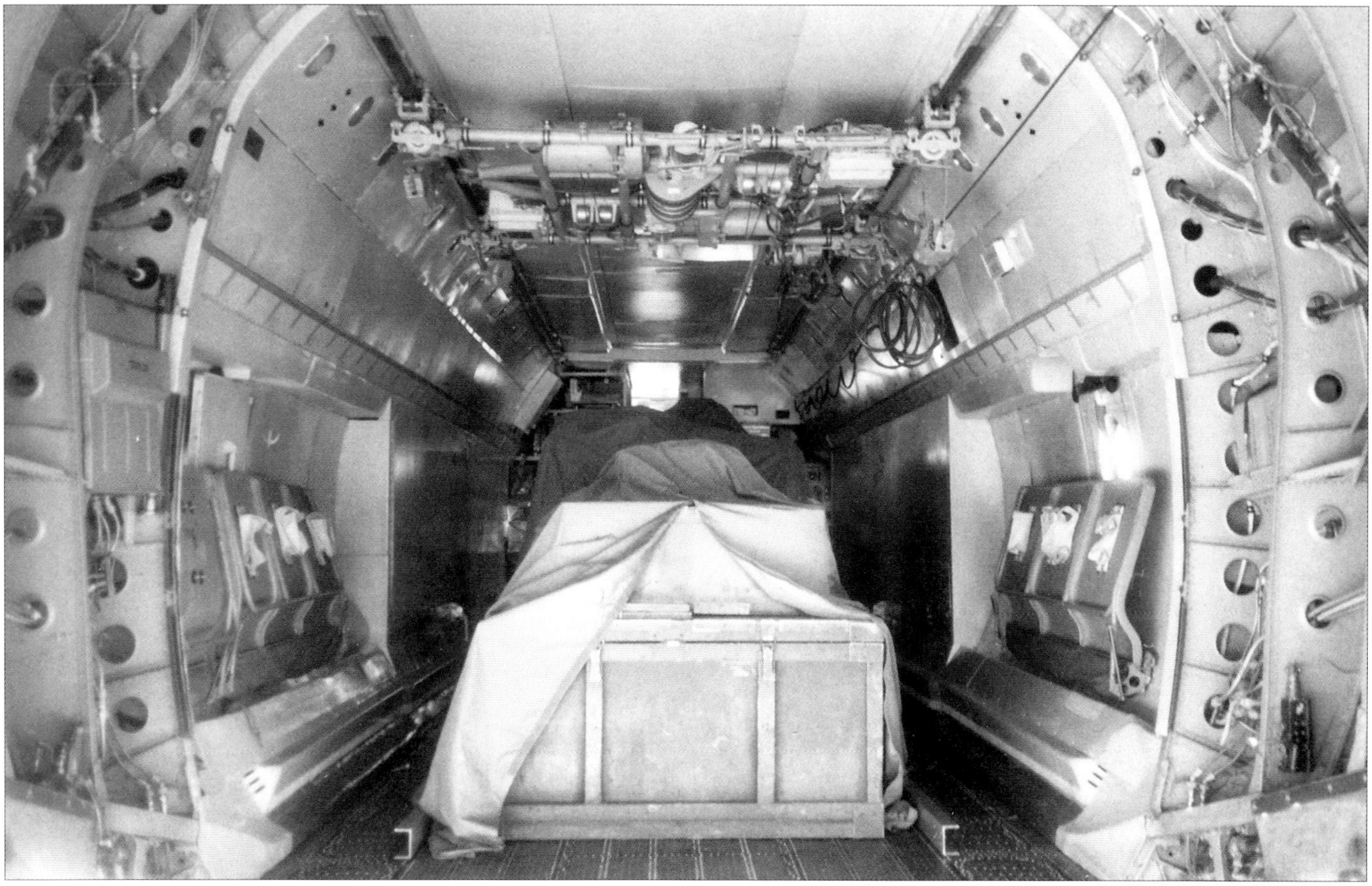

Above: The An-72P's main landing gear fairing features a cutout at the front on the starboard side for a UPK-23-250 cannon pod carried on a pylon. Two more detachable pylons are installed under the inner wings for carrying bombs or rocket pods. Note the ram air intake and outlet orifice of the fuel tank vent system in the wing/fuselage fairing.

Above left: The cabin of the An-72P prototype, showing the greatly reduced number of tip-up seats on this particular example. The overhead hoist is retained, as the aircraft can still be used for airlifting materiel (exemplified by these crates).

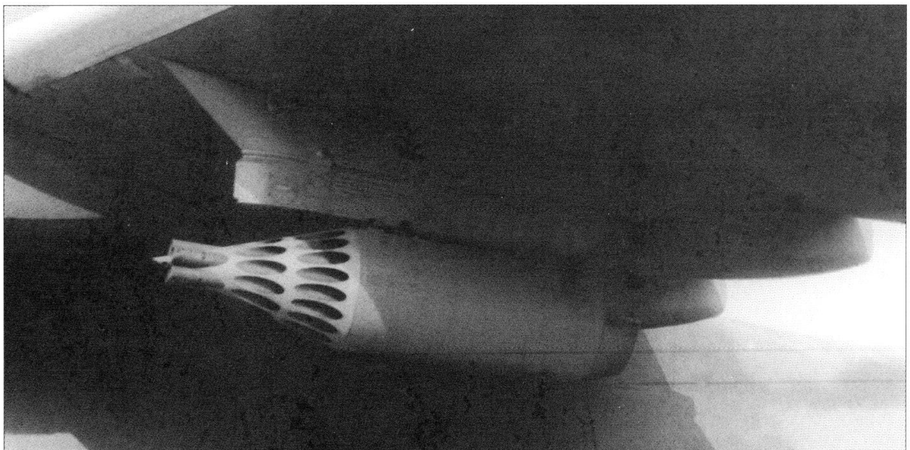

Below left: Bomb shackles on the An-72P's cabin roof above the cargo ramp can carry four 100-kg (220-lb) bombs – OFAB-100-120 high-explosive/fragmentation bombs in this case. Note also the overhead spotlight illuminating the loading area and the de-icing system hot air duct leading to the tail unit.

Right and above right: Close-up of the UB-32A rocket pods under the wings of the An-72P prototype.

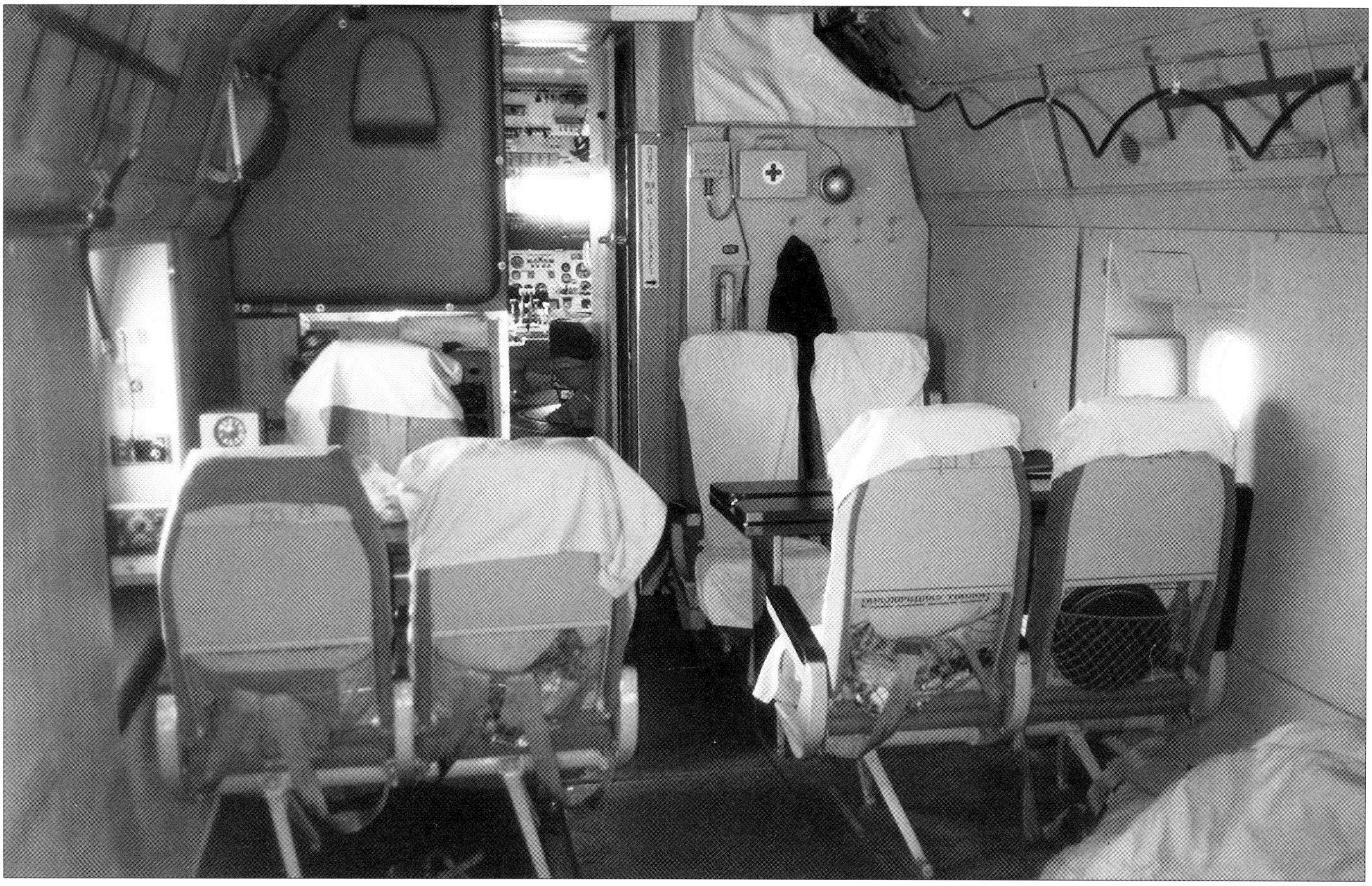

Above: Mission crew/passenger seats at the front of the freight hold of Aviacor's An-74 RA-74025 (c/n 365.470.95.905, f/n 1407) at the MAKS-93 airshow.

The VIP cabin ('main passenger's cabin') of An-74-200 UR-74055 (c/n 365.470.98.959, f/n 1710) at the MAKS-95 airshow.

Above: The cabin of the An-74TK-200 prototype, UR-74038 (c/n 365.470.97.933, f/n 1605) configured for passenger carriage at the MAKS-95. One of the overhead baggage bins on the port side is collapsed for demonstration purposes.

Another view of the An-74TK-200's cabin as the passengers see it on entering the aircraft. The interior is admittedly a bit... well, basic (the baggage bins look downright crude), but what it lacks in finesse it makes up for in functionality.

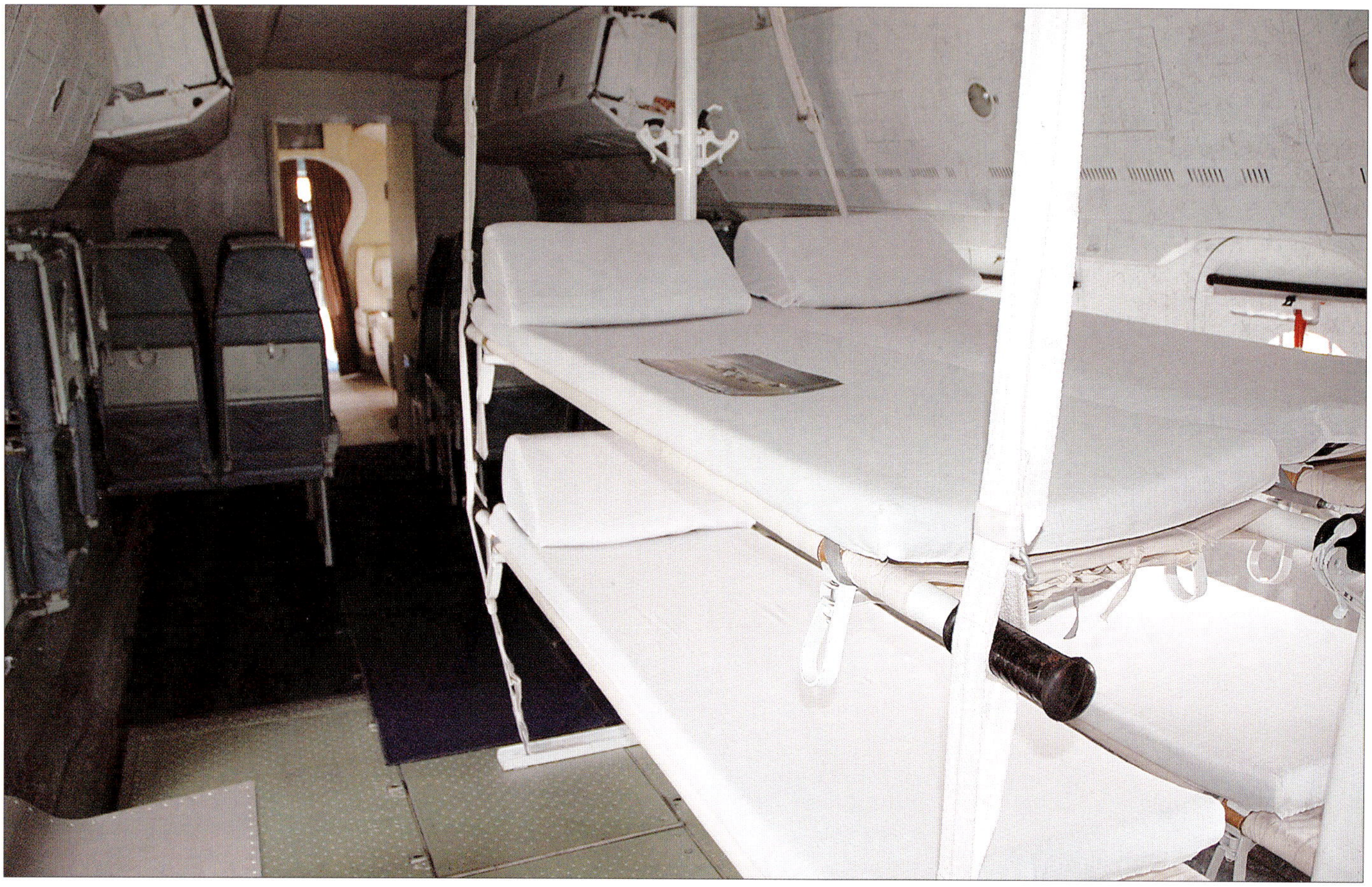

Above: At the Farnborough International 2002 airshow An-74TK-200 UR-74038 was shown with two tiers of stretchers at the rear of the cabin to demonstrate its Medevac capabilities. The passenger seats at the front of the cabin are retained.

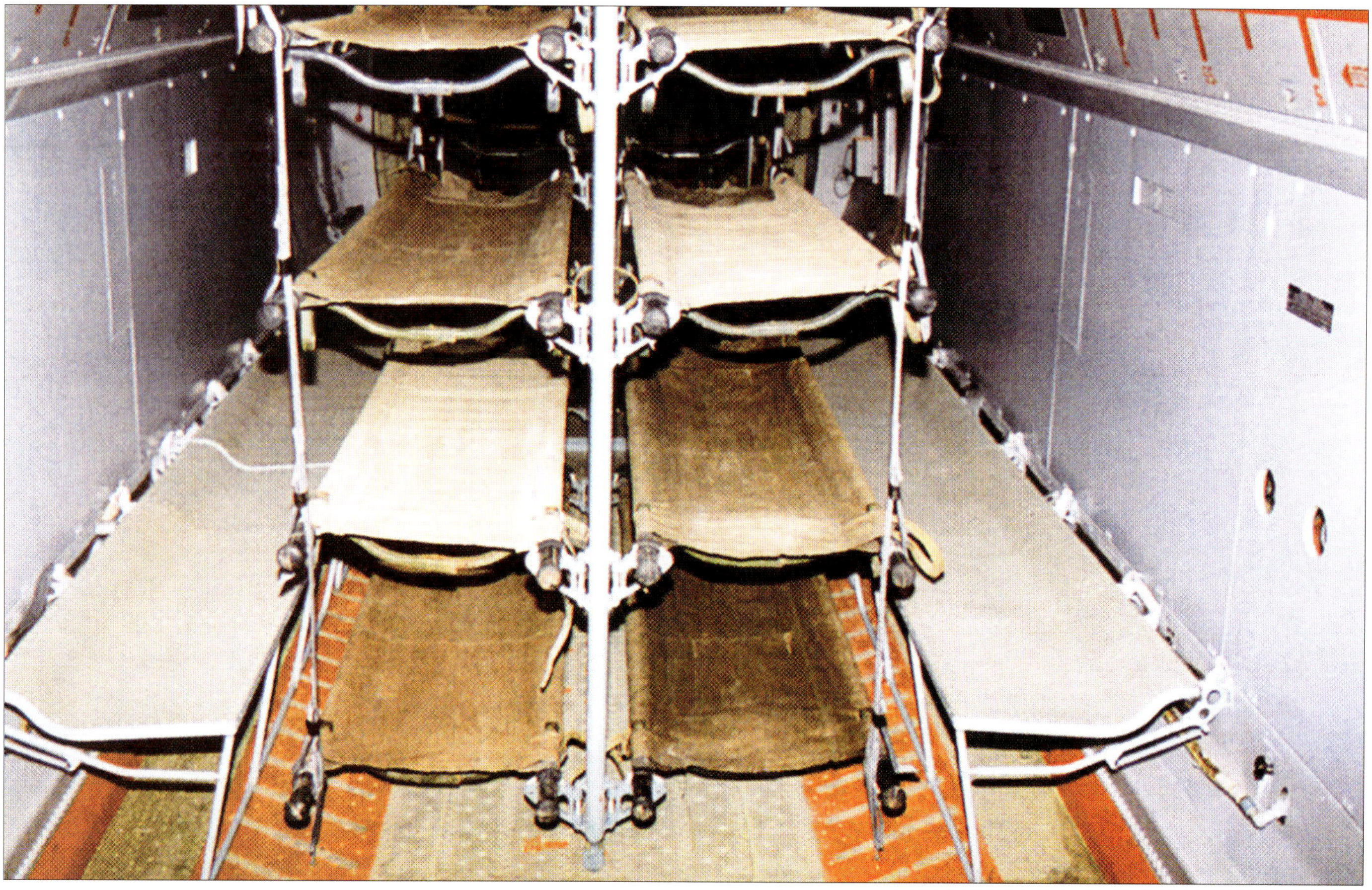

Here, for comparison, is a Casevac-configured Russian Air Force An-72. Four tiers of stretchers can be fixed to centreline uprights and nylon straps. This, however, renders the tip-up seats unusable – they have to be folded to provide passages along the walls and access to the patients.

Above: The cabin of the An-74TK-200 with the seats folded and the luggage bins collapsed. Roller tracks are fitted to the rear portion of the floor but, oddly, the rear cabin bulkhead is still in place. Note that the overhead lights built into the bottoms of the luggage bins remain operational when the bins are collapsed.

The cabin of the An-74TK-200 is rather claustrophobic, with very few windows. No, it's not a map over there on the forward bulkhead – just wall trim with a curious 'road map' pattern. The large forward emergency exit is just visible on the right.

Above: The first two rows of seats on the port side in the An-74TK-200's cabin feature a club-four arrangement with a table in between. The passengers in seats 1A and 2A are the luckiest of the lot; not only do they have window seats but they also enjoy the luxury of *six* cup holders! Boozers welcome!

This is how the rear portion of the cabin can be freed up for cargo in a combi layout. All you have to do now is move the rear bulkhead to a position aft of the remaining seats.

Left: An Antonov ANTK crewman folds the seats away in a demonstration of the An-74TK-200's interior flexibility.
Right: An extra Type III emergency exit is is provided on the port side of the An-74TK-200's rear fuselage. Note the area aft of it to be chopped out in an emergency.

Rear view of An-74TK-200 UR-74038, showing the modified vehicle loading ramp with pop-up steps, the extra step on the cargo ramp's trailing edge, the removable handrail and the carry-on luggage racks suspended from the ceiling aft of the cabin's rear bulkhead. Note the extended telescopic supports.

Above: The Nos 1 and 2 VIP cabins of An-74D RA-74048, with a cabin for the retinue further aft. The table in the No.2 cabin is positioned lengthwise and the tabletop folds to permit free passage.

Above: The No.1 VIP cabin of An-74D RA-74048, looking towards the nose, with a galley further forward. The in-flight entertainment system features five LCD TV screens.

encroaching on the freight hold. Leading-edge sweep 17° (constant on the short-fuselage/short-wing An-72 prototypes but reduced on the outer wings on production aircraft), anhedral 10° outboard of the engines, aspect ratio 11 on production aircraft. The wings utilise TsAGI airfoils with a high lift/drag ratio throughout the aircraft's speed range.

The wings are all-metal stressed-skin multi-spar structures made mostly of duralumin. On the short-fuselage/short-wing An-72 prototypes they consisted of three pieces: the centre section permanently attached to the fuselage and detachable wing panels with no sweepback on the trailing edges, plus GRP tip fairings. The stretched production version (and the An-74) has a five-piece wing structure, the detachable wing panels being divided into inner and outer sections outboard of the flaps; the outer sections feature modest trailing-edge sweep resulting in a kinked trailing edge. The large-span centre section carries the engine nacelles; titanium heat shields are provided on the upper surface. The wing/fuselage joint is covered by a fairing (see above) incorporating air conditioning system air intakes at the front and hinged dorsal access panels. The wing leading and trailing edge undersides feature numerous hinged panels made of CFRP for access to control runs, hydraulic lines, flap drive shafts, electric cables and so on.

The wings are equipped with powerful high-lift devices – double-slotted flaps on the centre section, triple-slotted flaps on the inner wing sections and three-section leading-edge slats (one section on each inner wing section and two on each outer section). The flaps move on external tracks enclosed by GRP fairings (two on each inboard/outboard flap). The inboard flaps are set directly, the outer flaps and the LE slats moving in concert; the inboard/outboard flaps are powered by different hydraulic systems for greater reliability. Flap settings are 10° inboard/25° outboard for

The tail units of the An-72P prototype (left) and a standard An-72 (c/n 365.720.10.952, right), showing the double-hinged rudder, the fin leading edge de-icer and the dielectric portions of the fin/tailplane fairing. The An-72P prototype has an extra APU in the rear fuselage with a fin root intake and a port side exhaust.

take-off and 60° inboard/40° outboard for landing.

Four-section electrohydraulically actuated spoilers/lift dumpers are installed on each inner wing panel; the innermost pair act as airbrakes and the outer two pairs are used for roll control. The short-fuselage/short-wing An-72 prototypes had four additional spoilers on the wing centre section aft of the engine nozzles. Two-section ailerons *(see Control system)* are installed on the outer wings.

Tail unit: Cantilever swept T-tail of all-metal stressed-skin construction. The vertical tail consists of a narrow fin and a large double-hinged rudder *(see Control system)*. Leading-edge sweep 33°30'.

The fin is a two-spar stressed-skin structure with a one-piece detachable leading edge doubling as a de-icer. The forward rudder segment is a one-piece metal structure while the rear segment is split, the upper half being made of GRP, with reduced trailing-edge sweep below the joint line.

The variable-incidence horizontal tail of trapezoidal planform comprises two stabilisers hinged to the fin's rear spar and one-piece elevators *(see Control system)*. It has an inverted airfoil with a flat upper surface. Leading-edge sweep 23°, no trailing-edge sweep, aspect ratio 3.44, taper 1.15. Each stabiliser is of two-spar construction with a so-called deflector (inverted leading-edge slat) which deploys when the flaps are selected fully down to prevent deep stall. A two-section GRP fairing at the top encloses the fin/tailplane joint; the pointed forward portion is fixed while the greatly bulged rear portion tilts together with the tailplanes as stabiliser incidence changes.

Landing gear: Hydraulically-retractable tricycle type, with free-fall extension in emergency. The nose unit features twin 720 x 310 mm (28.3 x 12.2 in) non-braking wheels and a combined steering actuator/shimmy damper. The four independent main units have single 1,050 x 390 mm (41.3 x 15.3 in) wheels equipped with hydraulic multi-disc brakes.

All landing gear struts are made of titanium and have oleo-pneumatic shock absorbers and levered suspension. The steerable nose unit can turn ±50° for taxying, enabling the aircraft to make a U-turn within a 15-m (49-ft) radius, and is controlled by a tiller on the port cockpit console. There are separate parking brake levers for the port and starboard wheels; these can be locked together.

The nose unit retracts forward, the main units inward into a large ventral GRP fairing which encloses both the mainwheel wells, the main gear fulcrum (main pivot) attachment fittings and the actuation gear. The main gear

Above: The centre fuselage of An-72 c/n 365.720.10.952, showing the main landing gear fairing. Note the open APU air intake, the bulged APU cowling and the APU exhaust surrounded by a steel heat shield.

Above: The starboard main gear units, showing the levered suspension and the hefty shock absorbers. Note the flat-top 'hubcaps' via which the wheels rest on the wheel well doors when retracted.

The nose gear unit has levered suspension and non-braking wheels of the same model as used on the Yakovlev Yak-40 feederliner. The lower AShS-UD communications blade aerial is visible further aft.

Above: Maintenance work is in progress on the starboard D-36 engine of an An-72; the forward pair of cowlings is open and the thrust reverser is deployed.

A view of the engine accessory gearbox and accessories through the lower rear pair of cowling doors.

struts have breaker struts retaining them in extended position but no uplocks, the mainwheels resting on the inner faces of the mainwheel well doors when retracted. Maximum landing gear transition speed is 345 km/h (214 mph).

The nosewheel well is closed by two lateral doors and a small rear door segment hinged to the oleo strut. The main units on each side have a large common main door attached to the fuselage keel beam, closing the wheel well, and small individual doors hinged to the oleos. All wheel well doors are made of CFRP; the larger doors open only when the gear is in transit.

Powerplant: The An-72 and An-74 are powered by two Lotarev D-36 Series 2A or D-36 Series 3A turbofan engines with a take-off thrust of 6,500 kgp (14,330 lbst) in standard atmosphere conditions and a cruise thrust of 1,600 kgp (3,530 lbst) at 8,000 m (26,250 ft) and Mach 0.75. The engine was developed by the 'Progress' Zaporozhye Engine Design Bureau (ZMKB Progress) and manufactured by the Zaporozhye Engine Factory (ZMZ, later Motor-Sich); it has a modular construction of 12 basic modules which can be replaced in service and makes large-scale use of titanium.

The D-36 is a three-spool turbofan with a single-stage transonic fan having 29 titanium blades with part-span shrouds (snubbers) and a parabolic spinner, a six-stage transonic low-pressure (LP) axial compressor featuring fixed inlet guide vanes, titanium discs/rotor blades, steel stator vanes, a seven-stage subsonic high-pressure (HP) axial compressor with variable inlet guide vanes, bleed valves at the 3rd and 4th stages, titanium blades on the first five stages and steel blades elsewhere, a low-smoke annular combustion chamber with 24 fuel nozzles and two igniters, single-stage HP and LP turbines with cooled blades, and a three-stage fan turbine. Each spool rotates in two bearings – that is, there are only six bearings (no inter-shaft bearings).

There are separate core and bypass nozzles (called rear support case and bypass duct respectively); the bypass duct is split into front and rear modules (called contravane case and intermediate case respectively). The contravane case features 49 stator blades and is reinforced with a composite liner to preclude uncontained fan failure; the fan blades are designed to withstand birdstrikes.

A ventral accessory gearbox is mounted on the intermediate case. Starting is by means of an SV-36 air turbine starter (*star**tyor** vozdooshnyy*) using compressed air from the APU, ground supply or cross-feed from the other engine.

Bypass ratio 5.6 in take-off mode and 6.2 in cruise mode; overall engine pressure ratio 20.2 at take-off power and 19.8 in cruise mode, mass flow 253 kg/sec (557 lb/sec) at take-off power and 148 kg/sec (326 lb/sec) in cruise mode. Turbine temperature 1,450°K at take-off power and 1,245°K at cruise power; maximum turbine temperature 1,510°K. Fan speed 5,400 rpm, LP spool speed 10,500 rpm, HP spool speed 14,170 rpm. Specific fuel consumption at take-off power 0.358 kg/kgp·h (lb/lbst·h), cruise SFC 0.649 kg/kgp·h. Length overall 3,470 mm (11 ft $4^{39}/_{64}$ in), width 1,541 mm (5 ft $0^{21}/_{32}$ in), height 1,711 mm (5 ft $7^{23}/_{64}$ in); dry weight 1,106 kg (2,438 lb).

The D-36 has a self-contained pressure-feed lubrication system, as well as a fuel flow control system and an electronic engine control system ensuring automatic starting and stable operation in all modes. The fuel flow control system maintains constant engine rpm in accordance with the throttle settings. The electronic engine control system monitors the engines' operating parameters (exhaust gas temperature, vibration levels and so on) and automatically throttles back the affected engine if any of these parameters reaches a dangerous level or the engine surges. Apart from manual control by the pilots, engine rpm may be set automatically by the SAU-72 automatic flight control system which includes an autothrottle.

The engines are mounted in nacelles attached to the wing centre section above and ahead of the wing leading edge and carried in truss-type bearers; the engine attachment lugs are mounted on the bypass duct

and rear support case. Each nacelle consists of a one-piece annular forward fairing incorporating a de-icer, two large cowling panels hinged at the top, three pairs of double cowling panels (each pair has three Camloc fasteners) and a fixed rear portion. The latter incorporates a thrust reverser which is part of the airframe, not the engine, and serves both the core flow and the bypass flow for maximum effect. Each thrust reverser has an aft-hinged main door and an internal blocker door aft of it which drops down against the wing's upper surface; together they direct the exhaust flow forward and up. The exhaust orifices have a flattened shape to spread the jet over the inboard flaps. The nacelles' forward portions and cowlings are made of GRP.

The An-74TK-300 is powered by two Muravchenko (ZMKB Progress) D-436T1 turbofans rated at 7,500 kgp (16,530 lbst) for take-off and 1,500 kgp (3,310 lbst) for cruise at 11,000 m (36,090 ft) and Mach 0.75. The D-436T is an uprated derivative of the D-36 incorporating various improvements, including a cascade-type thrust reverser on the bypass flow (for most versions). Bypass ratio 4.98, overall engine pressure ratio at take-off power 22.17, cruise SFC 0.617 kg/kgp·h, turbine temperature 1,520°K, dry weight 1,450 kg (3,200 lb). The engines are carried on underwing pylons in cylindrical nacelles with tapered front and rear ends; the thrust reverser cascades of each engine are covered by a translating cowl.

An-72 prototypes and initial production aircraft had a Stoopino Machinery Design Bureau TA-8V auxiliary power unit for self-contained engine starting, ground power supply and air conditioning. The TA-8V has a single-stage centrifugal compressor, a single-stage peripheral turbine and a 12-kW GS-12TO DC starter/generator. Dimensions, 1.368 x 0.701 x 0.717 m (4 ft 5$\frac{7}{8}$ in x 2 ft 3$\frac{19}{32}$ in x 2 ft 4$\frac{15}{64}$ in), dry weight with generator 216 kg (476 lb). Bleed air pressure 3.3 bars (47 psi), delivery rate 0.75 kg/sec (1.65 lb/sec), equivalent power 107 kW, fuel consumption 145 kg/h (320 lb/h). The APU can be started at altitudes up to 5,000 m (16,400 ft).

Later An-72s and An-74 variants feature a Stoopino Machinery Design Bureau TA-12 APU with a four-stage axial compressor, a three-stage axial turbine, a GS-12TO DC starter/generator and a 40-kW GT40PCh8B stable-frequency AC generator. Dimensions, 1.588 x 0.682 x 0.721 m (5 ft 2$\frac{1}{2}$ in x 2 ft 2$\frac{55}{64}$ in x 2 ft 4$\frac{25}{64}$ in), dry weight less generators 290 kg (640 lb). Bleed air pressure 4.9 bars (70 psi), delivery rate 1.6 kg/sec (3.52 lb/sec), equivalent power 287 kW, fuel consumption 250 kg/h (551 lb/h). The APU can be started at altitudes up to 7,000 m (22,965 ft).

The APU is installed in the starboard rear portion of the main gear fairing under a one-piece upward-hinged CFRP cowling, featuring an upward-opening rear-hinged dorsal intake door and a lateral exhaust surrounded by a steel heat shield. It is started, using 27V DC from a ground source or on-board DC batteries.

Control system: Powered dual controls with irreversible hydraulic actuators in all three control circuits and a manual emergency backup mode. Control inputs are transmitted to the actuators by conventional mechanical linkages (push-pull rods, cranks and levers).

Roll control is provided by two-section ailerons on the outer wings assisted by the outer two spoiler sections on each wing; the spoilers come into action when the control wheel angle exceeds 15°. The smaller inboard aileron sections are controlled directly and used in high-speed flight; the outer sections join in at low speeds. In the event of an engine failure with more than 10° flap the outermost spoiler section on the live-engine side is deployed automatically to offset the lift asymmetry caused by the thrust asymmetry; ten seconds later it sinks back over another ten seconds, giving the pilot time to react. Each aileron section is hinged on two brackets. The inboard sections have geared tabs; the port inboard aileron also has an electrically operated trim tab.

Pitch control is provided by one-piece elevators with both aerodynamic balancing (horn balances) and mass balancing. Each elevator is hinged on four brackets and incorporates a geared tab and a trim tab. Additionally, the aircraft is balanced fore and aft by changing the tailplane incidence.

Directional control is provided by a double-hinged rudder whose rear segment is split. The metal lower rear rudder section is controlled directly by the rudder pedals and features a trim tab at the root; the GRP upper section joins in at low speeds by means of a hydraulic drive; this enhances flight safety and obviates the need for an artificial-feel mechanism. The one-piece forward rudder segment hinged to the fin torsion box deflects automatically to offset the thrust asymmetry in the event of an engine failure but is locked until the flaps are extended. Each rudder segment is carried on three brackets.

The aircraft has an SAU-72 automatic control system (*sis**tem**a avtoma**tich**eskovo oopravl**en**iya*) including an autopilot; the system's directional control channel operates as a yaw damper. The autopilot servos are connected to the control runs in parallel and may be disengaged pyrotechnically if they jam. The servos feature overriding clutches, allowing the pilots to take corrective action when the autopilot is engaged.

Electrically actuated gust locks are provided to prevent damage to the control system by high winds while the aircraft is parked. The rudder and ailerons are locked neutral and the elevators fully down to offload the hydraulic actuator. For safety reasons, throttle movement is mechanically limited if the locks are engaged; the locks are inhibited with the landing gear in no-load position.

Fuel system: The wing torsion box (centre section, inner and outer wings) is divided into seven integral fuel tanks. Total fuel capacity for the production-standard An-72 and An-74 is 16,250 litres (3,575 Imp gal). The fuel tanks are split into four groups (Zero, One, Two and Three); the Group Three tanks are service tanks (to be precise, each of them features a service section from which fuel is fed to the respective engine). The Group Zero tank holding 2,395 litres (526.9 Imp gal) is a reserve tank filled for long-range flights only.

Normally the port and starboard halves of the system are isolated, but a cross-feed valve enables each engine to draw fuel from any group of tanks. The APU is fed from the port engine's fuel line or by a special APU supply pump installed in the starboard Group Three tank.

The An-72/An-74 has single-point pressure refuelling; the refuelling panel is located on the port side of the main gear fairing. Refuelling to maximum capacity at 4.5 kg/cm^2 (64 psi) takes about ten minutes. Fuel grades used are Russian T-1, TS-1 or RT kerosene, Western JP-1, Jet A-1, Avtur or equivalent; the addition of water crystallisation inhibiters (grade 'I' special fluid or tetrahydrofurfurol alcohol) in winter enables refuelling at ambient temperatures of +5°C (+41°F) or lower. The refuelling and fuel usage sequence is controlled automatically by the fuel metering/control system or manually by the crew.

A vent system is provided; venting is done via the Group Zero tank which is connected both with all other tanks and with the atmosphere. Fuel jettisoning in flight is possible via the engines' fuel delivery lines by means of jettison cocks located on the starboard side of both engine nacelles, using the transfer pumps and delivery pumps. Defuelling is also possible via the drain valves found in each tank.

Hydraulics: Two separate hydraulic systems (port and starboard) which power the control surface actuators, high-lift devices, spoilers, landing gear, nosewheel steering mechanism, wheel brakes, thrust reversers, entry door emergency actuator (or, on the An-74D/An-74TK-300, the airstair door), cargo ramp/doors, telescopic rear supports and windshield wipers.

Both systems use AMG-10 oil-type hydraulic fluid (*aviatsi**on**noye **mahs**lo ghidravl**ich**eskoye*). Both systems are powered by

Above: The flightdeck of an An-72 configured for a crew of three (note the curved track for the flight engineer's centreline seat at the bottom of the picture). Note also the individual weather radar displays with rubber sunblinds on the captain's and co-pilot's consoles.

The overhead circuit breaker panel and the master warning panel ahead of it, with no fewer than 96 strip lights.

Above: The captain's instrument panel and side console of An-72 CCCP-72936 (c/n 365.720.60.642, f/n 0607). Note the nosewheel steering tiller on the side console and the red parking brake handles to the right of the control column.

The co-pilot's instrument panel and side console of the same aircraft. The weather radar displays feature a different type of sunblind. Note the moving-map display (MMD) on the central control pedestal operated by the co-pilot who acts as the navigator.

The flightdeck of an early An-74 – again with an MMD on the central control pedestal. The centre portion of the panel is occupied by engine instruments.

variable-capacity engine-driven pumps. Each system has its own hydraulic tank; the two tanks are manufactured as a single module and equipped with a pressurisation system.

The port hydraulic system includes an electrically-powered pump unit and a hand-driven pump as back-up hydraulic power sources. The electric pump unit ensures the operation of hydraulic equipment on the ground during maintenance and tops up the parking brake's hydraulic accumulator. The hand-driven pump ensures the opening/closing/sliding of the cargo ramp when electric power is off and is used for refilling the hydraulic tanks.

A cross-feed valve allows the engine-driven pumps and electric pump unit to serve all hydraulically-powered equipment; if one pump fails, the other pump can serve both systems, providing there is no hydraulic leak.

Electrics: The electric system operates the avionics, part of the de-icing system, fuel system components (pumps and cocks) and cargo handling equipment. Primary 200/115V/400 Hz three-phase AC is supplied by two 30-kVA engine-driven generators or a 40-kVA generator driven by the APU. Secondary power sources are two 2-kVA step-down transformers providing 36V/400 Hz three-phase AC and two 6-kW rectifiers providing 27V DC.

All electric subsystems operate in parallel, each using its own group of distribution buses. Electric power management is automated; if a power source fails, its distribution buses are automatically switched to one of the surviving power sources. Overload protection devices automatically exclude a failed power source or damaged section of circuitry.

Three 27V (25 A·h) DC batteries are housed in the port rear portion of the main gear fairing and accessed via an upward-hinged CFRP cover. Backup three-phase AC power is provided by a 0.8-kVA static converter fed by the batteries. A 27V DC ground power receptacle is installed in the starboard front portion of the main gear fairing.

De-icing system: The de-icing system ensures icing protection at ambient temperatures down to –30°C (–22°F). The wing and tail unit leading edges and fuel tank venting system air intakes are de-iced by hot air from the air conditioning system; the engine air intakes are de-iced by hot air bled from the third HP compressor stage. Electric de-icing on the flightdeck windshield, pitot heads and static ports; the windshield is provided with wipers for removing the snow and melting ice. Alcohol de-icing on the observation blisters and flightdeck windshield.

A radioactive isotope icing detector is installed on the port side of the fuselage nose. The system is activated either automatically by the icing detector but can be deactivated only manually.

Fire suppression system: Two single-shot fire extinguisher bottles charged with $114V_2$ grade chlorofluorocarbon (CFC) are provided for fighting fires in the engine nacelles and in the APU bay. The crew is alerted by a fire warning system with flame sensors and an engine overheating warning system. The fire suppression system has a two-stage operating algorithm; the first shot is triggered automatically by flame sensors or manually at the discretion of the crew, the second shot manually only.

The fire extinguishers are actuated electrically from the overhead circuit breaker panel in the flightdeck. Two impact sensors installed under the fuselage trigger all fire extinguishers automatically in a wheels-up landing. Portable fire extinguishers charged with 115V grade CFC are provided for fighting cabin and flightdeck fires, including electrical fires.

To maximise fire resistance the airframe incorporates firewalls and fireproof materials. Systems and equipment are carefully laid out to minimise the fire hazard and drains are provided at locations where flammable liquids might accumulate.

An inert gas pressurisation system featuring nitrogen bottles is provided on military versions (the An-72) to pressurise the fuel tanks and reduce the hazard of explosion if hit by enemy fire.

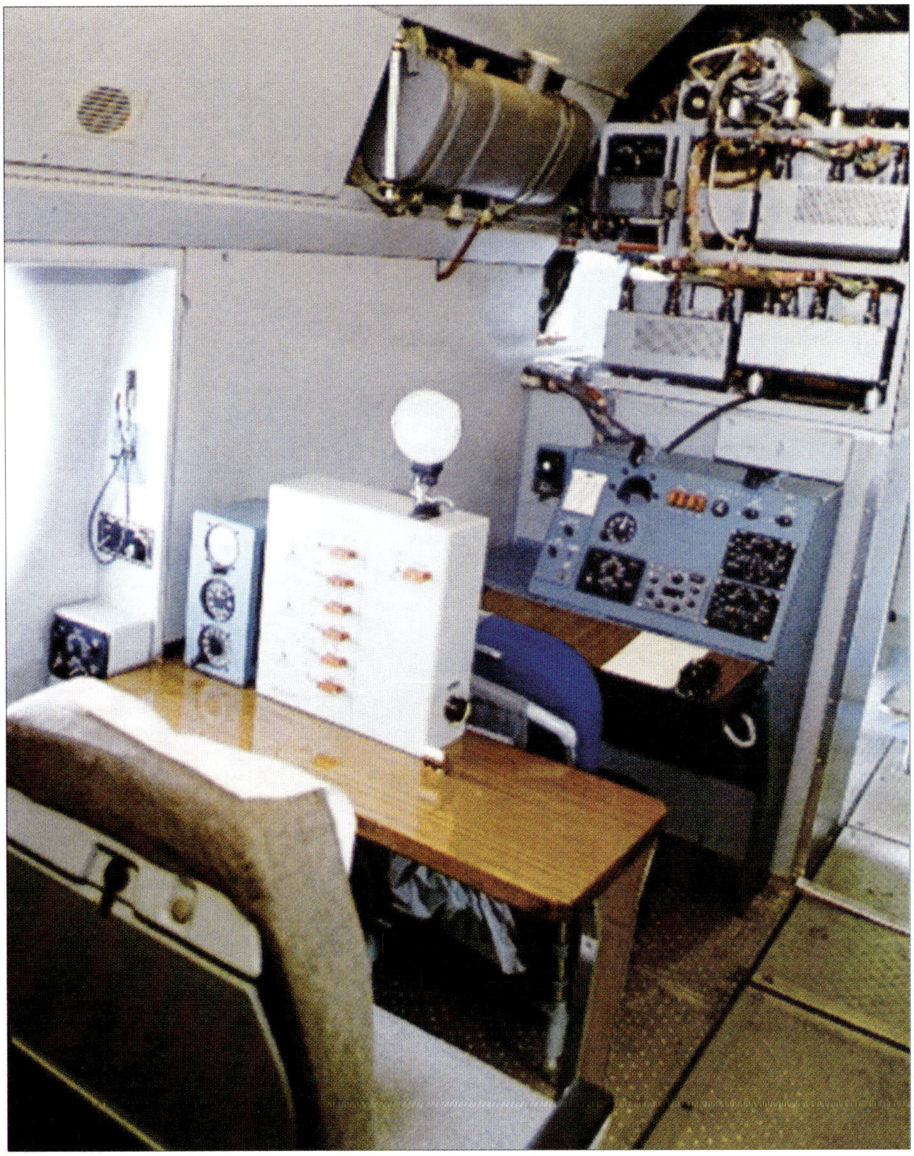

The hydrologist's (observer's) station of an An-74, with a further mission crew workstation further ahead (just aft of the entry door). Note the alcohol tank for the observation blister's de-icing system

Air conditioning and pressurisation system: The greater part of the fuselage is pressurised and air-conditioned by air bled from the engines' 4th HP compressor stages in all operational modes, including ground idle, or the APU. There are two air conditioning systems (port and starboard) serving the freight hold/passenger cabin and the flightdeck respectively. The starboard ACS can operate in refrigeration mode if the freight hold is used for carrying perishables.

Cabin air pressure and temperature are maintained automatically or may be set manually. Maximum cabin pressure differential 0.49 kg/cm² (7.1 psi). Warning lights are provided for monitoring the systems' operation.

Pneumatic system: A separate system is provided for pressurising the avionics bays and adjusting tyre pressure. The pneumatic system maintains a pressure differential of 0.9-1.1 kg/cm² (12.8-15.7 psi) at all flight altitudes and in all engine operation modes. Tyre pressure is adjusted to suit the aircraft's weight and runway class to facilitate operations from unpaved airstrips. The air is bled from the ACS.

Oxygen system: An oxygen system is provided to protect the crew and passengers against hypoxia in the event of decompression or against smoke and toxic fumes in the event of a fire. The system comprises two 10-litre (2.2 Imp. gal.) oxygen bottles for the cabin, with distribution manifolds and connectors for individual oxygen masks, and stationary breathing apparatus for the flight crew. Operation time at least 3 hours for decompression and at least 15 minutes for smoke protection.

An augmented supply of oxygen is provided on the An-72S VIP aircraft in all-passenger configuration; the oxygen bottles are mounted on the rear cabin roof above the cargo ramp.

Above: The forward section of the flightdeck on An-74 RA-74025. Note the radar display replacing the MMD on the central control pedestal.

The navigator's station of the same aircraft.

Avionics and equipment: The An-72/An-74 is fully equipped for all-weather day/night operation, including automatic and semi-automatic flight assisted by an autopilot. Special attention was paid to flightdeck ergonomics in order to reduce the crew workload.

a) Navigation and piloting equipment: The An-72 has an SAU-72 automatic flight control/landing system comprising an autopilot and a Mal'va Doppler-based automatic navigation system. The Doppler antenna is located under the main gear fairing, offset to starboard. The SAU-72 permits automatic ICAO Cat I blind landing (decision altitude 60 m/200 ft, horizontal visibility 800 m/2,600 ft). A Gradiyent navigation/weather radar is installed in the nose, with separate navigation and weather displays.

The flight avionics include a multi-channel speed and altitude data system, a metre-waveband long-range radio navigation system, a decimetre-waveband short-range radio navigation system and distance measuring equipment.

The flight instrumentation features a master warning panel above the windscreen displaying red lights for critical failures and yellow lights for non-critical failures to minimise time spent on monitoring instruments and equipment.

b) Communications equipment: HF communications/command link radios for long-range air/ground communications served by a forward-pointing probe aerial on the fin top fairing. Short-range VHF air/air and air/ground communications radios with AShS-UD blade aerials on the forward fuselage underside and atop the fin. An emergency radio is fitted to assist in locating the aircraft in the event of an off-field forced landing in localities lacking ground navaids. An intercom is provided.

c) IFF system: SRO-1P Parol'-2D (*izdeliye* 62-01) IFF transponder with characteristic triangular aerials located on top of the radome and on the tailcone (just aft of the rudder trailing edge).

The aircraft also features ATC transponders enabling flights in and outside the CIS. These transmit the aircraft's registration, speed and altitude for presentation on ATC radar displays and may operate in 'Mayday' mode.

d) Data recording equipment: MSRP-64-2 or MSRP-64M-2 flight data recorder and Mars-BM cockpit voice recorder. The FDR captures 12 parameters, including barometric altitude, indicated airspeed, roll rates, vertical and lateral G forces, control surface deflection and throttle settings, as well as gear/flap transition etc. All recorders have armoured shells to ensure survival in a crash.

e) Lighting equipment: Port (red) and starboard (green) navigation lights at the wingtips, white tail navigation light at the aft end of the fin top fairing. Retractable PRF-4M landing/taxi lights on the sides of the main landing gear fairing at the front. White MSL-3 rotating anti-collision beacons under the main landing gear fairing, offset to port, and at the top of the fin. Tail unit inspection light buried in the rear fuselage near inspection window to enable icing checks. Primary and back-up cabin, flightdeck and instrument panel lighting. Floodlights in the freight hold roof above the cargo ramp to assist loading/unloading at night; overhead lights in the hold.

Above: The pilots' instrument panels and central control pedestal of An-74D RA-74048.

The navigator's station of the same aircraft; the map table tips up for access to the seat. Note the aircraft's registration on a sticker at the top of the instrument panel on the right.

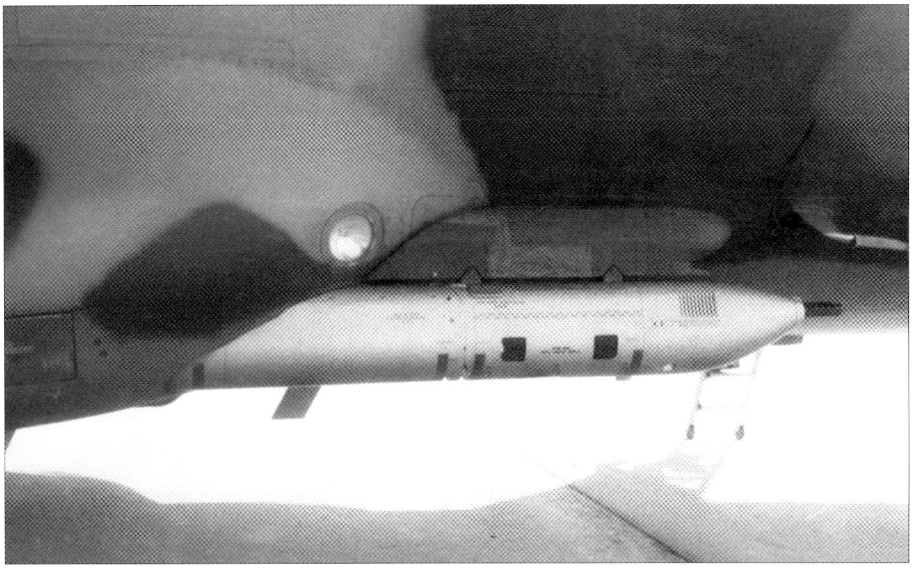

Above: The UPK-23-250 cannon pod on the fuselage pylon of the An-72P prototype.

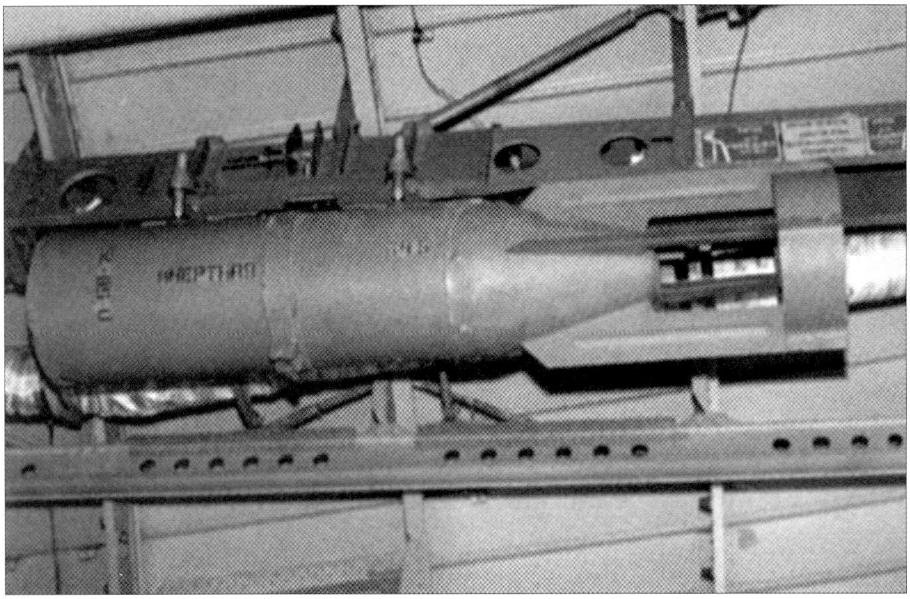

An inert OFAB-100-120 high-explosive/fragmentation bomb on one of the four internal shackles of an An-72P.

Accommodation and cargo handling/paradropping equipment: The basic An-72 has tip-up seats along the freight hold walls and removable centreline seats for 68 passengers. It can carry 57 parachutists; 'traffic lights' and a siren are provided for initiating the drop sequence. Provision is made for 24 stretcher patients, 12 seated casualties and a medical attendant in CASEVAC configuration.

In cargo configuration the aircraft can carry single, packaged or containerised/palletised loads, including up to four UAK-2.5 containers or four PAV-2.5 pallets each weighing 2,500 kg (5,510 lb). Items weighing up to 2,500 kg can be airdropped by parachute extraction system.

For lifting items of cargo from the ground or from a truck-bed and arranging them in the cargo cabin the An-72/An-74 features an overhead hoist with a maximum lifting capacity of 2,500 kg travelling along rails mounted on the freight hold ceiling. The electrically powered hoist has a system of pulleys and can handle containers and pallets measuring up to 1.90 x 2.44 x 1.46 m (6 ft 2$\frac{13}{16}$ in x 8 ft 0 in x 4 ft 9$\frac{31}{64}$ in) and other bulky items. For cargo handling operations with the cargo ramp slid forward under the fuselage, two hydraulically-powered telescopic supports normally stowed in the rear ends of the main gear fairing are deployed to stop the aircraft from falling over on its tail.

The freight hold floor features numerous threaded holes into which cargo tie-down lugs can be screwed; these are otherwise stored in special canvas bags attached to the walls and the holes closed by screw-in plugs. The cargo is secured by nets, chains and turnbuckles. If necessary, roller conveyors can be installed on the floor for container/pallet handling and paradropping, allowing a single cargomaster to move loads weighing up to 2 tons (4,410 lb). Special graphic symbols stencilled on the floor indicate the required placement of cargo items for CG reasons and assist the loading of wheeled vehicles.

Two or four detachable vehicle loading ramps can be hooked up to the trailing edge of the cargo ramp with the ramp fully lowered; on convertible variants (An-74TK-100/-200/-300) they may be replaced with boarding steps.

The An-72S executive aircraft has a VIP cabin at the front with a club-four seating arrangement and four-abreast seating for 20 in the back or, alternatively, a cargo cabin for carrying a high-ranking officer's jeep or saloon car. The VIP cabin is separated from the rear cabin by a solid bulkhead with a door.

The An-74 can carry eight mission staff in combi role, in two rows of seats, with tables, and with two bunks, one on each side of cabin aft of seats. A hydrologist's workstation with an observation blister can be located on the port side aft of the entry door. Provision is made for a wardrobe, a galley and a lavatory.

The An-74TK-100/-200 has up to 52 passenger seats four-abreast in double units folding up against the cabin walls for all-cargo or combi layouts and racks for carry-on baggage suspended from the cabin ceiling above the cargo ramp. Alternative configurations are 20 passengers plus 4.5 tons (9,920 lb) of cargo, 12 passengers plus 6 tons (13,230 lb) of cargo, or 10 tons (22,045 lb) of cargo. The seat modules and baggage shelves may be removed altogether for all-cargo operations. The An-74TK-300 seats up to 60 passengers four-abreast in all-economy configuration.

Rescue equipment (An-74): Three inflatable lifeboats and life jackets are carried on overwater missions.

Armament (An-72P): One UPK-23-250 gun pod with a 23-mm (.90 calibre) Gryazev/Shipoonov GSh-23 double-barrel cannon. The GSh-23 weighs 51 kg (112 lb) and fires 200-gram (7.06-oz.) projectiles; rate of fire is 3,200 rounds per minute and muzzle velocity 700 m/sec (2,296 ft/sec). Two pylons under the extremities of the wing centre section permit carriage of bombs of up to 500 kg (1,100 lb) calibre or UB-32 rocket pods holding 64 S-8 80-mm (3.15-in) folding-fin aircraft rockets. Four 100-kg (220 lb) bombs can be carried on shackles at the rear of the freight hold and dropped with the cargo ramp in paradropping position.

Ranging and weapons aiming is by means of an electro-optical (TV) sight looking through a window under the forward portion of the main landing gear fairing, offset to port.

Chapter 4

The Twins in Service

As already mentioned, the An-72 was built as a military transport aircraft, while the outwardly identical An-74 was delivered primarily to commercial operators. Of course, there were exceptions; many An-72s were sold to commercial operators in post-Soviet times, and military An-74s are also known.

An-72 deliveries to the Soviet Air Force commenced in 1986. As was the case with some other Soviet Air Force transports, most An-72s were quasi-civil and wore full Aeroflot colours, although a few examples carried a tactical code along with a civil registration. Comparatively few An-72s wore overt military markings; such aircraft were usually light grey overall in the manner of Soviet Air Force An-12s and An-26s, although a few combined the star insignia with basic Aeroflot colours.

Actually the Aeroflot livery was often non-standard. Concurrently with the An-72's service introduction the Ministry of Civil Aviation made an attempt to liven up the fleetwide standard livery devised in 1973, which consisted of a white upper fuselage and vertical tail, a grey lower fuselage, grey wings and tailplanes, and a blue cheatline with a blue pinstripe underneath. Not wishing to waste his imagination on inventing a completely new livery, someone suggested painting the vertical tail blue with a broad white horizontal stripe on which the Soviet flag was superimposed in the usual place, and sometimes the outer wings were also blue. This did improve the appearance a bit, and the modified livery was worn by various aircraft, although such machines were usually military or operated by the flying divisions of MAP and other ministries. For some reason the blue/white tail livery stuck mostly to the An-72, at least 18 aircraft being painted in this fashion.

The An-72's suitability for paradropping cargo and personnel was rather limited due to the narrow cabin incompatible with large cargo pallets, which made paradropping combat vehicles impossible, and the strong downwash aft of the wings. Also, problems were experienced with the sliding cargo ramp which sometimes jammed as it was opened for paradropping. Even more importantly, airborne assaults were usually planned as massive vertical envelopment operations, and the larger An-12 and IL-76 were better suited for this.

Hence the An-72 was used mostly in the VIP transport role, earning the nickname *ghene**rahl**'skiy samo**lyot*** (translates loosely as 'Big Brass Flyer'). However, it would be fair to say that the time of its production entry also contributed to this. Had it not been for the collapse of the Soviet Union and the ensuing political and economic chaos of the 1990s, the An-72 would have been built in greater numbers for the Soviet Air Force and would probably have succeeded the An-26 in service with regular airlift regiments.

Anyway, the first operational unit to receive the type was one of the two regiments constituting the 8th ADON (Special Mission Air Division) at Chkalovskaya AB. This unit was by far the largest An-72 operator. Its *Coalers* took military and government delegations all over the Soviet Union and were also used by General Headquarters delegations inspecting Soviet/Russian troops stationed in Eastern Europe – the Northern Group of Forces (Poland), the Western Group of Forces (East Germany, and subsequently post-reunification Germany), the Central Group of Forces (Czechoslovakia) and the Southern Group of Forces (Hungary). Overall grey An-72s wearing star insignia but (apparently) no tactical

Russian Air Force/978th VTAP (Military Airlift Regiment) An-72 '35 Blue' (c/n unknown) sits at Klin-5 AB near Moscow in non-flyable condition. The starboard engine cowlings come from An-72 CCCP-72937.

Russian AF An-72 '09 Blue' (c/n 365.720.93.875, f/n 1209) was in the static park during the third 'open house' at Kubinka AB on 14th May 1994. Note the nose flash in the Russian flag colours (white/blue/red).

Above: An-72S CCCP-72916/'02 Red' (c/n 365.720.40.525, f/n 0502) shares the flight line at Vladimirovka AB, Akhtoobinsk, with a grey-painted sister ship in transport configuration and several Sukhoi Su-24 tactical bombers. The concrete hardstand is augmented by 'patches' composed of perforated steel planking.

It is not common for Russian Air Force An-72s to combine blue/white tails with star insignia. An-72S '01 Red' (c/n unknown) is a fairly frequent visitor to Zhukovskiy and is seen here a minute after landing on runway 30 on 21st August 2003, bringing military top brass to the MAKS-2003 airshow.

Above: 978th VTAP An-72 CCCP-72937 (c/n 365.720.70.688, f/n 0704) sits in storage at Klin-5 AB and is non-flyable, as indicated by the missing APU intake door. For some reason this aircraft and '35 Blue' (see page 87) have switched cowlings! Note the black anti-soot stripes aft of the engine nozzles and the red-tipped tailcone.

An-72S CCCP-72931 (c/n 365.720.70.695) shares the hardstand at Kubinka AB with An-12BP '17 Red' (c/n 5342810) on 11th April 1992, the base's first 'open house'. The air intake covers boldly carry the f/n 0510, which is actually An-72 CCCP-72921 (c/n 365.720.40.581)! The nozzle covers carry this aircraft's proper f/n, 0707.

Above: An-72S RA-72938 (c/n 365.720.70.693, f/n 0706) taxies out for take-off at Savasleyka AB near Nizhniy Novgorod, with some of the resident fighters in the background. The aircraft sports a white tail and a unit badge aft of the flightdeck. Note the uniformly grey radome lacking the customary darker grey tip.

The same aircraft caught by the camera as it touches down at Savasleyka AB; the spoilers are already deployed. Note the scarecrow in the foreground clad in a Russian Army trenchcoat and winter cap. Makes you wonder who it is intended to scare – birds… or spotters (by posing as a sentry)?

Above: An-72S RA-72947 (c/n 365.720.90.803, f/n 0905) sits at Chkalovskaya AB, grounded by the lack of the radar – a typical result of the problems with spares procurement in post-Soviet times. The air intake covers are marked '947-11', possibly indicating the jet was previously coded '11 Red'.

Russian Air Force/8th ADON An-72S RA-72946 (c/n 365.720.90.801, f/n 0904) completes its landing run at Ghelendjik, bringing visitors to the Hydro Aviation Show 2002 from Chkalovskaya AB.

Above and below: Russian Air Force An-72P '27 Blue' (c/n unknown) in well-weathered three-tone camouflage is seen on final approach, carrying a cannon pod but no FFAR pods; note the red Federal Border Guards identification stripe on the tail. The red anti-collision lights are noteworthy.

codes were also spotted near Chkalovskaya AB in 1986, but these were not 8th ADON aircraft and were undergoing trials at the local GNIKI VVS facility.

Other Soviet Air Force units operating the An-72 were stationed at Klin-5 AB (Moscow Defence District), Kishinyov (Carpathian DD), Alma-Ata (Kazakhstan, Central Asian DD) and Kiev (the Ukraine, Kiev DD). Ostaf'yevo AB lying just outside Moscow's southern limits became home to a handful of An-72Ss supporting the operations of the Soviet/Russian Navy General Headquarters.

In November 1999 an Independent Airlift Squadron was formed within the structure of the Strategic Missile Forces (RVSN – *Ra**ket**nyye voy**ska** strate**gich**eskovo nazna**chen**iya*) to support the headquarters of this offensive arm. The unit was equipped with An-72Ss sporting blue/white tails.

Another military operator of the type was the Border Guards Directorate of the notorious KGB (State Security Committee). In post-Soviet times the Border Guards Directorate was reorganised as the Federal Border Guards (FPS – *Fede**rahl'**naya pogra**nich**naya **slooz**hba*). This remained an organisationally separate service until it merged back into the FSB (*Fede**rahl'**naya **slooz**hba bezo**pahs**nosti* – Federal Security Service, the KGB's successor) in 2004. In addition to regular transport and VIP examples (based at Moscow/ Sheremet'yevo-1 and Leningrad-Pulkovo, among other things), which entered service back in Soviet days, the FBG took delivery of a dozen or so An-72P patrol aircraft. The jets were operated by the FBG's Arctic and Far Eastern Air Groups; as well as the North Caucasian Special Border District.

Above: An-72P '22 Blue' (c/n unknown) in basic Aeroflot colours with appropriate 'Ан-72П' nose titles and

Centre and above: '24 Blue' (presumably c/n 365.760.91.830, f/n 1007), another camouflaged FBG An-72P. Note the canvas covers over the observation blister and the cannon pod in the lower photo.

Above: The An-74 prototype, CCCP-72003, visits one of the Soviet research station in Antarctica as part of the type's Polar trials, December 1988.

The unarmed An-72s invariably wore full Aeroflot livery (and usually had white tails), while the combat version usually had military markings, although two Russian An-72Ps were quasi-civil – at least for a while. Some of the An-72Ps were in basic Aeroflot colours, others wore two- or three-tone tactical camouflage. A characteristic feature of the FBG's An-72Ps, camouflaged or not, was the Border Guards insignia – a horizontal red band on the tail at about half its height (on camouflaged helicopters this band is white).

The An-72 was easy to fly and well liked by its crews who were quick to appreciate its benign handling and good STOL properties. Once the teething troubles had been overcome, the aircraft showed quite a good reliability record. On the other hand, landing speed limits and other limits had to be observed to avoid damaging the structure. Also, the An-72's higher complexity as compared to its turboprop stablemates required a greater maintenance effort and higher skills on the part of the ground crews; the latter were not very happy about the high-set engines which required tall ladders and work platforms to reach them.

Russian Air Force and FBG An-72s saw action during both Chechen Wars (1994-96 and 1999-2001). Suitably configured transport examples from Chkalovskaya AB were used for CASEVAC duties along with IL-76s and other transports, flying to Groznyy-Severnyy airport and Khankala AB. One such aircraft was captained by Lt. Col. Aleksandr Kozlov, with Lt. (sg) Artyom Sayetovich as co-pilot and Lt. Col. Igor' Kashantsev as navigator. The An-72 made as many as seven sorties per day, taking wounded personnel from field hospitals, where they had received first aid, to Saratov, Samara and Moscow (notably the Russian MoD's Central Hospital named after N. I. Boordenko) for further treatment. A case is on record when a CASEVAC-configured An-72 flew 52 sorties within 17 days without a single malfunction.

North Caucasian Special Border District An-72s and An-72Ps home-based at Stavropol'-Shpakovskoye airport. These flew medical and support sorties, delivering materiel to the war zone. This is where the camouflage worn by the An-72Ps was most welcome.

In the Russian Far East, the An-72Ps were involved in a different war – the war against the fish mafia. Illegal fishery in Russia's 200-mile economic exclusion zone (EEZ) was a major source of ill-gotten gains, and the poachers had second-hand Japanese fishing cutters at their disposal. These were fast and well-equipped craft which the FBG's patrol boats often had trouble intercepting. Thus the An-72P was a most welcome addition to the FBG inventory. Until then the Border Guards had to rely on obsolete piston-engined IL-14s (which were rapidly becoming extinct), An-26 turboprops and even Yakovlev Yak-40 trijet feederliners chartered from Aeroflot's Far Eastern Civil Aviation Directorate. All of these aircraft were unarmed and had nothing with which to press the message home to the poachers that they were under arrest. The FBG's Mil' Mi-8IV, Mi-8MIV-2 and Mi-24 assault helicopters were armed but too slow.

An atmospheric shot of An-74 CCCP-72003 in Antarctica. The aircraft is refuelled by a TZA-7,5-500A fuel bowser based on a MAZ-500A 4x2 cabover lorry, with a GAZ-3705 civilian tracked amphibian standing alongside.

Above: Wearing the short-lived registration CCCP-72200, the An-74 prototype (ex/to CCCP-72003) is pictured at Novaya Zemlya in February 1988 during a sortie in support of a Soviet-Canadian cross-polar ski expedition. An Aeroflot Mi-8, an IL-14 and a TZA-7,5-500A in yellow Aeroflot colours are visible in the background.

On several occasions the An-72Ps had to fire in anger at intruders attempting to get away. Such vessels were not in a hurry to identify themselves and could just as easily turn out to be not fishermen at all but intelligence vessels (which often intruded into Soviet territorial waters in the Cold War years to reconnoitre the sensitive military installations on the Pacific coastline). Thus, at 0800 hours on 21st February 2001 the FBG patrol boat RNS *Paghella* detected an unidentified Japanese-built vessel which ignored orders to stop and made off at full speed.

An An-72P was summoned to the help from Petropavlovsk-Kamchatskiy (Yelizovo airport), detecting the intruder, but all attempts to establish radio contact with the ship proved fruitless. At 0935 hours the aircraft fired warning shots with its GSh-23 cannon, but the ship's captain would not heed the warning. At 1000 hours the An-72P made the first real attack and scored a hit, but was forced to return to base soon afterwards.

Around 1700 hours a US Navy Lockheed EP-3E Orion reconnaissance aircraft contacted the *Paghella*, informing the crew of the intruder's whereabouts; by then the corvette RNS *Kamchatka* was also involved in the operation. At 2340 hours the same An-72P located the target again. The scenario was repeated: after firing warning shots, which were ignored, the aircraft attacked. Only then did the ship's captain respond to the radio calls, stating that some of his men were wounded; but even then he stubbornly refused to stop the ship.

A second An-72P took over the chase at 0143 hours on 22nd February. Then the target ship established radio contact with one of the pursuing FBG ships, finally identifying herself as M/V *Albatross-101*; the captain again told there were wounded personnel aboard, there was a fire on board and the ship's hull had been holed. The *Paghella* and *Kamchatka* headed towards the *Albatross-101*, intending to extend help (and make a bust, of course); yet she changed course again in a determined attempt to escape from the EEZ. Not until more warning shots were fired did the captain finally give up; the cutter stopped and the crew hastily abandoned ship, whereupon the *Albatross-101* sank in 5,000 m (16,400 ft) of water. The crew, who were arrested and taken to Petropavlovsk-Kamchatskiy, could give no plausible explanation of why the ship was there.

As with nearly all aircraft in Russian Air Force service, An-72 operations suffered from the economic downturn affecting the nation in the 1990s. Actually the An-72 was more

A Moldovan An-72 chartered for supporting one of the annual Paris-Dakar rallies takes off from a dirt airstrip somewhere in Africa, raising an almighty trail of dust.

Above: An-74TK-200 UR-74038 demonstrates its ground manoeuvrability by making a U-turn on the runway at Kiev-Gostomel' on 15th September 2002 during the second Aviasvit-XXI airshow.

UR-74038 gives a demonstration of its STOL capabilities, coming to a halt with spoilers deployed and engines at full reverse. The black anti-soot markings on the wings are a standard feature.

affected than many other types because, apart from fuel shortages, there were political complications into the bargain. The airframe and engines were produced in the Ukraine, with which Russia was then at odds over a number of economic and military issues. Spares procurement thus turned into a real problem, forcing much of the fleet to be mothballed (this applied to the transport and VIP versions, but not to the An-72P). This is one of the reasons why some Russian Air Force An-72s were sold abroad in the late 1990s.

The career of the An-72's commercial 'twin brother', the An-74, got off to a troubled start. The aircraft had just received its type certificate in 1991 and deliveries to Aeroflot were just beginning when the Soviet Union collapsed. Aeroflot detachments which took delivery of the Antonov twinjet were the Krasnoyarsk Civil Aviation Directorate/Noril'sk United Air Detachment, Tyumen' CAD/Nadym UAD and Yakutian CAD/Kolyma-Indigirka UAD (the latter was home-based in the town of Cherskiy). A few were also delivered to various industrial enterprises.

The An-74 often gives spirited performances at airshows, as exemplified by this roll executed by UR-74038 at the 2002 Aviasvit-XXI.

At first the An-74 seemed to justify its originally intended Polar aviation specialisation. The first operational missions the type had to fly were associated with Arctic and Antarctic research. The first one – actually a rescue mission – came in early 1986 when the as-yet sole prototype (then still registered CCCP-780334 and equipped with the original short radome) was in the middle of its trials programme. An expedition led by the well-known adventurer Dmitriy Shparo had made an unprecedented crossing on skis over the Arctic ice from one drifting research station, the SP-26 (SP = ***Sev**ernyy **pol**yus* – North Pole), to another – the SP-27 – across the so-called Pole of Relative Inaccessibility. Several members of the expedition suffered from severe frostbite and required medical attention; an airlift operation was needed. The 1,400-m (4,590-ft) ice runway at SP-27 was suitable for An-12s, but a week before the expedition reached the station the ice floe split, leaving the SP-27 with just 600 m (19,685 ft) of usable runway. This was too short even for the IL-14, never mind the An-12; the An-2 could use a 600-m runway but lacked the range to reach the SP-27, which was then 1,650 km (1,024 miles) from Chokurdakh, the nearest airfield on the mainland, and 1,000 km (621 miles) from Zhokhov Island. The An-74 was the only aircraft capable of doing the job.

It took a maximum of effort to obtain MAP clearance for the mission. The point was that, as already mentioned, the An-74 then existed as a single and not yet fully tested prototype, and nobody wanted to accept the responsibility, should anything go wrong. Eventually the OKB disguised the operation as 'operational testing in the conditions of the High North' – which was not too far from the truth, as such tests were indeed planned.

On 9th March 1986 CCCP-780334 departed Kiev, flown by a crew comprising captain Sergey A. Gorbik, first officer Vladimir Lysenko, navigator Nikolay I. Malash and flight engineer Sergey I. Zhovnir. The mission crew included chief engineer Anatoliy Romanyuk, expedition head Igor' D. Babenko (Vice-Director of the OKB's flight test facility) and journalists from Moscow and Kiev; there were 14 occupants in all.

After a night stop on Dixon Island the aircraft arrived in Cherskiy on 10th March. There the crew undertook a series of tests, trying to obtain the shortest possible take-off run at the anticipated take-off weight. The best results (350-380 m/1,150-1,250 ft) were obtained by starting the take-off run with normal take-off flap (10° inboard/25° outboard) and deploying the outer flaps to their maximum setting of 40° as the aircraft accelerated to 140 km/h (87 mph). This technique was kept secret from the head office in Kiev for fear of a ban being imposed on the whole mission.

On 11th March the team relocated to Chokurdakh at the suggestion of Yachmenyov, head of the Kolyma-Indigirka UAD (a squadron of this air detachment was based in Chokurdakh). That day the aircraft made a flight to Zhokhov Island for the purpose of setting up a staging area there; the local 1,000-m (3,280-ft) runway located on the ice of a frozen bight was hitherto used only by An-2s. After leaving a 7,500-litre (1,650 Imp gal) supply of kerosene drained from the aircraft's tanks on the island for the flight back from the SP-27 the crew returned to Chokurdakh. The following day, however, they were in for a nasty surprise: Vice-Minister of Aircraft Industry A. S. Systsov had sent a telegram prohibiting the flight to the ice station.

The reason was clear: Yachmenyov was pursuing his own ends. He was the author of an alternative rescue operation plan involving six An-2s which were to reach the SP-27 in three stages, four of the aircraft carrying fuel drums to top up the others. Two pairs of aircraft with a supply of fuel would await the return of the third pair at the intermediate stops. Hence he had given the Antonov team the cold shoulder, but could not turn them down because the team enjoyed support from Minister of Civil Aviation Boris P. Boogayev. However, no sooner were the 'competitors' off to Chokurdakh than he 'stabbed them in the back', sending a telegram to Systsov to the effect that landing the An-74 on the ice floe was too dangerous and winning support from the Vice-Minister.

All the team was authorised to do at this point was to make a pass over the SP-27 and airdrop supplies – which they did. The Mal'va navigation system guided the An-74 to the target with pinpoint accuracy and the free-fall drop was accomplished; still, no permission was forthcoming.

The situation was resolved the following day in a most unusual manner. It turned out that Dmitriy Shparo had a friend in high places – the son of Yegor K. Ligachov, a high-ranking figure in the Communist Party Central Committee. The Deputy Editor-in-Chief of the *Komsomol'skaya Pravda* daily (which had organised Shparo's expedition) called Ligachov Jr. from Chokurdakh, and the wheels

Above: The ill-starred An-74 CCCP-74002 (c/n 365.470.70.682, f/n 0703) of the Yakutian CAD/Kolyma-Indigirka UAD at Moscow/Sheremet'yevo-1 in 1991, with the characteristic 'mushroom' satellite building in the background. This aircraft was lost in a fatal crash in Lensk on 16th August 1991.

were set in motion. Junior complained to his dad, who promptly telephoned Systsov and gave him the old what-for! After that, authorisation at the ministerial level was obtained in no time at all!

On 14th March the An-74 made the first flight to the SP-27, picking up eight of the expedition's 15 members. The rest were airlifted the following day – on the second try; the first attempt was foiled by an oil leak in the starboard engine, the aircraft returning to Chokurdakh where it transpired that the oil filler simply had not been closed properly after refilling the tank the night before. On 17th March the aircraft departed Chokurdakh for Moscow via Salekhard.

In late 1987 the same aircraft, by then fitted with a new radar and reregistered CCCP-72003, travelled all over the Soviet Union's Arctic coastline, flying to the Zemlya Frantsa-Iosifa (Franz Joseph Land) archipelago and Chukotka (an area in the Russian Far East) and covering more than 2,000 km (1,240 miles) in the polar night. The aircraft also flew sorties to the ice stations SP-28 and SP-30, assisting in evacuating the personnel of the latter. In 1988 CCCP-72003 took a ski expedition to the Antarctica; this time the aircraft again had to undertake a medical sortie, taking a Soviet polar researcher who had fallen ill to Argentina for treatment.

As the Soviet Union ceased to exist, in the ensuing turmoil Arctic research had to be put on hold and the An-74's intended Polar mission was forgotten. Worse, this turmoil (namely the disintegration of traditional economic co-operation ties between the Soviet republics) put the continued production of the An-72/An-74 in jeopardy. Even though the airframe and engines were of Ukrainian make, many avionics components (such as landing gear struts and wheels) were subcontracted out to Russian enterprises. In view of the rampant inflation and scant buying power of the new national currencies, the Khar'kov State Aircraft Manufacturing Co. had to pay for components delivered from Russia in kind – that is, in the form of whole aircraft or spares for same. On the other hand, An-74 production in Omsk never began in earnest because all Omsk-built examples were assembled from parts manufactured in Khar'kov. As for the plans to build the type at the Arsen'yev Aircraft Production Association in the Russian Far East, as already mentioned, not a single An-74 was ever produced there.

Being the sole aircraft type then in production in Khar'kov (that is, until the An-140 twin-turboprop regional airliner came on the scene), the An-72/An-74 was of special importance for the Ukraine. The need to tailor the machine to customer requirements, coupled with the customers' meagre budgets, led the Antonov ANTK and the plant to offer 'low-cost' versions of the An-74 differing from the baseline model only in freight hold layout and equipment. Theoretically, this would assure a large influx of orders – especially from third-world nations. In reality, the attempts to export the An-74 have had only modest success; according to the Ukrainian Ministry of Industrial Policy, 34 examples were sold abroad in 1992-97, the largest single order (for twelve An-74T-200s and An-74TK-200s) being signed by Iran in 1995. (Sales of second-hand aircraft don't count.) At a flyaway price of around US$ 12.5 million, most customers found the An-74's Western counterparts, such as the British Aerospace 146/Avro RJ, more attractive due to their better operating economics and wider product support/maintenance network. Some prospective customers, such as Afghanistan and Nicaragua, were forced to cancel their orders, being torn apart by civil wars.

The numerous airlines large and small formed within the CIS after the disintegration of the 'all-Union' Aeroflot saved the day. Few could order large numbers of aircraft, but together they kept the production line going. The relatively cheap aircraft produced close at hand was just the right thing for airlines which were in need of fleet renewal but could not afford Western types due to high import duties and other reasons. Gazpromavia eventually became the biggest An-74 operator within the CIS, flying both domestic/international cargo charters and VIP charters – even in support of the Russian government. For example, a delegation from the Russian constituent republic of Tatarstan headed by Academician Dmitriy S. Likhachov, Chairman of the Russian State Council, which visited Copenhagen on 22nd-24th October 1997 was brought to Copenhagen-Kastrup by An-74D RA-74012. The aircraft, which did not wear Gazpromavia titles, was decorated for the occasion with the galloping horse logo of the KamAZ automobile factory located in Tatarstan.

Other Russian air carriers operated the An-74 on cargo charters abroad, too; thus, Bashkirian Airlines had services to Antalya and Izmir (Turkey) and to Larnaca (Cyprus) every two weeks. The An-72 even won recognition in the Baltic states which have generally done their best to get rid of Soviet types inherited from Aeroflot. Here, Enimex of Estonia has been steadily expanding its fleet of second-hand An-72s, even operating joint services with Western carriers.

Operational experience showed that the An-74's STOL capability remained largely unwanted because most airports do not practice steep approaches and climbouts, having a standard and rather flat glideslope angle of 3°40'. There were, however, certain missions where the type's STOL and rough-field capability proved invaluable. Since the early 1990s the An-74 has been actively used in support of the annual Paris-Dakar rallies, carrying sports marshals, the equipment of TV crews and other paraphernalia. Moldovan-registered civil examples were the first to do so, but since the mid-1990s Gazprom has been winning Dakar rally support contracts for many years in a row. Aircraft involved in the Dakar airlift sport the same characteristic stickers as the cars and trucks taking part in the event, plus stickers explaining the nature of the cargo (for example, TV FRET – French for 'TV CARGO') and occasionally sponsors' logos as well.

The *Coaler*'s STOL performance and toughness have also made it a suitable aircraft for peacekeeping and humanitarian airlift missions (under the auspices of the United Nations or otherwise) – though, strangely enough, only lately has it begun flying such missions. During the 2002 war against the al-Qaeda terrorist network and the Taliban militia in Afghanistan the Iranian Republican Guard's An-74T-200s occasionally delivered humanitarian cargos to Kabul. In 2004, Enimex An-72-100s have flown UN missions to Afghanistan (as part of the effort to overcome the aftermath of the long civil war) and to Sierra Leone in support of the United Nations Mission in Sierra Leone (UNAMSIL). The two An-74Ps operated by the Russian Ministry for Civil Aid and Protection (EMERCOM) also participate occasionally in disaster relief missions.

The An-72/An-74 has earned a reputation as a fairly reliable and safe aircraft. Nevertheless, attrition did occur, and partly due to hardware failures. The first accident with the type was at Kiev-Gostomel' in the early 1980s, involving the first prototype An-72 (by then reregistered CCCP-72004 No.1) which was extensively damaged in a hard landing. There were no fatalities but the aircraft was withdrawn from use and eventually rebuilt as the first prototype An-71, its former registration passing to a production An-74.

The first fatal crash occurred in Lensk, Yakutian Autonomous SSR, on 16th September 1991. An-74 CCCP-74002 of the Yakutian CAD/Kolyma-Indigirka UAD (c/n 365.470.70.682, f/n 0703) was making a cargo flight. The An-74's normal take-off weight is 34,800 kg (76,720 lb); under exceptional circumstances it may be increased to 37,800 kg (83,330 lb). On that day the aircraft had been overloaded so gravely that the actual TOW reached an impressive 41 tons (90,390 lb). The An-74 stood up to the challenge, becoming airborne (albeit with some difficulty) and starting a climbout. Then, however, the crew made a fatal mistake, retracting the flaps prematurely. With the greatly increased weight, the aircraft could no longer maintain the climb, losing altitude and hitting a hillside; all 11 occupants were killed. The almost brand-new aircraft, which was manufactured on 3rd January 1989, had logged only 923 hours 40 minutes' total time and 552 cycles. Interestingly, it used the ATC callsign CCCP-87136 on the day of the crash instead of its proper registration (the 87xxx block is allocated to the Yak-40).

On 23rd October 1994 An-72 RA-72960 (c/n 365.720.93.865, f/n 1203) operated by the FBG's Arctic Aviation Group suffered a hydraulic failure shortly after taking off from Vorkuta, Komi Republic, en route to a remote border post. The crew elected to return to Vorkuta but the flaps could not be deployed. Landing too fast at 290 km/h (180 mph), the aircraft overran the runway and came to rest with the port main gear collapsed. Due to the extensive structural damage to the lower fuselage and port wing the aircraft was declared a write-off.

On 10th December 1996 An-74-200 RA-74037 of Vostsibaero (c/n 365.470.98.950, f/n 1705) was taking off from Mirnyy, Yakutia, when the starboard thrust reverser deployed uncommandedly shortly before rotation speed. Veering off the runway, the aircraft collided with a brick building housing high-voltage transformers; a small fire broke out but was quickly extinguished. None of the eleven crew and passengers suffered anything worse than bruises. It turned out that the 'Thrust reverser unsafe' warning light had illuminated as the jet lined up for take-off but the crew had dismissed it as a false alarm. Again, the almost new aircraft manufactured on 28th April 1995 was damaged beyond repair, with only 369 hours and 176 cycles.

At 2134 hours on 23rd December 1996 another FBG/Arctic Aviation Group An-72 (identity unknown) captained by Senior Inspector Pilot Col. Vladimir Talanov crash-landed on Zemlya Frantsa-Iosifa, inbound from Vorkuta via Sredniy (= Middle) Island. The aircraft, which was delivering supplies and personnel to Border Post Nagoorskaya, suddenly yawed to the left a few moments before passing the runway threshold and hit a snow berm. Of the eight crew and 16 passengers, both pilots, the ground technician and another crew member and five passengers (including a child) received various injuries. The casualties were taken by a Royal Norwegian Coast Guard Aérospatiale Puma helicopter to Longyear, the administrative centre of the Spitsbergen archipelago; two of them required treatment in a hospital in Tromsø on the Norwegian mainland.

On 22nd December 1997 An-72 ER-ACF (c/n 365.720.94.888, f/n 1307) belonging to the Moldovan airline Renan went missing over the Atlantic Ocean off the coast of Angola. There is strong suspicion that the aircraft was shot down by Angolan Air Force fighters after refusing to land after being intercepted. The war against the UNITA guerrillas was still on at the time, and the An-72 was probably suspected of being on an arms trafficking flight for the UNITA. On the other hand, the UNITA was notorious for wantonly shooting down civil aircraft flying cargo charters in Angola.

On 6th October 2000 Centrafricain Airlines An-72 TL-ACW (c/n 365.720.90.796, f/n 0902) was damaged beyond repair in a wheels-up landing at Luzamba, Angola. The latest accident involving the type occurred on 21st April 2002 when An-72-100 ES-NOP of Enimex (c/n 365.720.10.905, f/n 0101) was written off in a crash landing at Wamena, Papua New Guinea.

As already mentioned, the An-74 (An-72 production has ended by now) is still of major importance for the Ukrainian aircraft industry. Fresh orders for this sturdy and versatile aircraft keep coming up, the most recent ones being from the Egyptian Government and Libya. By a strange twist of fate, the fact that customers were generally pleased with the An-74 has hampered its improvement and upgrading. Luckily, the Antonov ANTK and the Khar'kov State Aircraft Manufacturing Co. were not too late in realising this and set about bringing the aircraft in line with today's requirements. An extensive redesign of the 20-year-old aircraft would be too costly; still, the designers and manufacturers of the aircraft did the best they could. The result was the An-74TK-300, which traded the unwanted STOL performance for better operating economics.

Above and below: Two views of An-74TK-200 UR-74038 turning onto finals to Farnborough's runway 27 after a demonstration flight at the Farnborough International 2004 airshow in July 2004.

Chapter 5

Coalers Worldwide

Despite being produced in modest numbers, Antonov's twinjet transports have seen service in almost all parts of the world – Europe, Asia (including South-East Asia), Africa and Latin America. The Aeroflot and Soviet Air Force examples were distributed between several of the new CIS republics after the break-up of the Soviet Union, and CIS operators of the An-72/An-74 family will be dealt with first.

For each republic, operators are listed in alphabetical order, with each airline's two-letter International Air Transport Association (IATA) designator and three-letter International Civil Aviation Organisation (ICAO) designator where applicable. Aircraft no longer operated by the respective carrier are shown in italics in the fleet lists (except when the airline itself no longer exists or *all* of its *Coalers* have been sold or retired). For aircraft leased to other carriers, only the last known lease is indicated for reasons of space.

RUSSIA

• **Alliance Avia [–/NZP]** based at Zhukovskiy operates a small number of cargo and passenger aircraft, including five Antonov twinjets. Most of them are leased from Yamal Airlines and retain basic Yamal livery with ALLIANCE AVIA titles and 'AA' tail logo.

Registration	Version	C/n	F/n	Notes
RA-72918	An-72	365.720.40.548	0504	Leased from Yamal Airlines by 8-03; basic Aeroflot c/s, blue/white tail
RA-74020	An-74TK-100	47195014	0104P?	Khar'kov shipset 1810
RA-74027	*An-74-200*	*365.470.96.920*	*1507*	*Leased from Yamal Airlines 1-12-00 to 1-12-03; basic Yamal c/s*
RA-74043	An-74-200	365.470.96.923	1508	Leased from Yamal Airlines ?-00; basic Yamal c/s
RA-74052	An-74-200	365.470.98.944	1702	Leased from Yamal Airlines ?-01; basic Yamal c/s

• **Aviacor [–/VCR]**, the flying division of the Samara aircraft factory of the same name, operated two An-74s, RA-74025 (c/n 365.470.95.905, f/n 1407) and RA-74041 (c/n 365.470.96.924, f/n 1509), from Samara-Bezymyanka airfield. The airline suspended operations in late 1995 after a landing accident involving RA-74041. This aircraft was ultimately repaired and updated to An-74-200 standard for sale to Sibaviatrans, while the other *Coaler* was sold to RAF-Avia after conversion to an An-74TK-100 as YL-RAF in April 2001.

• **Aviaenergo [–/ERG]**, the Zhukovskiy-based flying division of the United Energy System of Russia JSC (*RAO Yedinaya energheticheskaya sistema Rossii*, the electric power monopoly), bought An-74 RA-74040 (c/n 365.470.97.930, f/n 1602) from Klyuch Air in 1996. Unlike most of Aviaenergo's fleet, the aircraft never received full company livery with the characteristic bright yellow/red/green bands and 'Electric Eagle' logo on a grey tail, wearing basic blue/white Aeroflot colours with red Aviaenergo titles and a red lower rudder half. Sometime before 1998 it was leased to the Angolan carrier Transaérea. In 1999 the aircraft was leased first to East Line and then to Shar, Inc.

• **Bashkirian Airlines** (*Bashkirskiye avialinii*) **[V9/BTC]** operated five An-74s based in Ufa.

Registration	Version	C/n	F/n	Notes
RA-74014	An-74	365.470.98.968	1807	
RA-74015	An-74	365.470.98.969	1808	Leased to Shar, Inc., ?-03
RA-74020	*An-74*	*47195014*	*0104P?*	*Khar'kov shipset 1810 Leased briefly in 2001*
RA-74046	An-74	365.470.97.935	1606	
RA-74047	An-74	365.470.97.941	1610	
RA-74048	An-74D	365.470.98.943	1701	VIP configuration, Bashkortostan titles. Leased to 2nd Sverdlovsk Air Enterprise in 2002

Four of the aircraft in the list had been acquired from the late Shonkar airline absorbed by BAL in 1997, originally retaining basic red/white Aeroflot polar colours with white tails and no titles but subsequently gaining the attractive BAL livery. However, being strictly a passenger carrier, Bashkirian Airlines were unable to efficiently manage a freighter fleet. Hence in 1999 the carrier streamlined its fleet by transferring the An-74s to a newly-formed division, TAB – ***Trahnsport**naya avi**ah**tsiya Bashkorto**sta**na* (Bashkirian Cargo Aviation). The latter is a wholly-owned subsidiary of BAL, which in turn is 100% owned by the state.

The fifth aircraft, RA-74048, was one of two VIP jets used by Bashkirian President Murtaza Rakhimov; it had basic BAL colours but wore 'БАШКОРТОСТАН' (Bashkortostan) titles.

• Established in 1993 as a cargo charter carrier, Moscow-Domodedovo based **East Line [P7/ESL]** has since grown into a major airline with both cargo and passenger services. The constantly changing fleet included a single An-74, RA-74040, briefly leased from Aviaenergo in 1998 and wore basic Aeroflot colours with small East Line titles. Additionally, RA-74047 was leased from Bashkirian Airlines in 1999.

• The **Flight Research Institute named after Mikhail M. Gromov (LII)** in Zhukovskiy operated An-72 '03 Red' (c/n 365.720.60.610, f/n 0603) converted into a navigation/automatic landing systems testbed.

• **Gazpromavia Ltd. [4G/GZP]**, the flying division of the powerful Gazprom corporation controlling Russia's natural gas industry, has built up a fleet of 12 An-74s by consolidating the industry's initially many flying divisions (some are still formally independent). The aircraft are based at Ostaf'yevo, a Naval Aviation base just south of Moscow, where Gazpromavia opened a small but very modern passenger terminal in 2003.

Above: An-74-200 RA-74052 (c/n 365.470.98.944, f/n 1702) was operated by Alliance Avia in basic Yamal Airlines colours (note the small Yamal titles aft of the larger observation blister). It is seen here at its home base of Zhukovskiy in August 2001.

Seen here in the static park of the MAKS-93 airshow, RA-74025 (c/n 365.470.95.905, f/n 1407) was one of two An-74s to wear this smart livery of the Samara-based Aviacor aircraft plant. It now serves with RAF-Avia of Latvia as YL-RAF.

Above: Seen on the eastern apron at Moscow-Domodedovo on 25th November 1998, Aviaenergo An-74 RA-74040 (c/n 365.470.97.930, f/n 1602) still has 'Polar' rudder colours. Note the windowless plug replacing the large rear blister. The sticker under the forward blister is a leftover from a lease to Transaérea of Angola.

VIP-configured An-74 RA-74011 (c/n 47136013, f/n 1809 – or 0103P?) wears full Shar, Inc. (ШАР) colours augmented by bold Cyrillic 'Gazprom' titles. The owner's

Most of them are pure freighters or convertible utility aircraft that can seat up to 52, used for delivering urgent cargo or shifts of personnel. There are a few exceptions, though; RA-74012 has a 12-seat VIP interior, while RA-74005 has been refitted as an ambulance aircraft. Most of the An-74s wear full Gazpromavia livery, though the colours and especially the tail logo vary. The logo comes in three versions: a Roman G with a small tongue of flame (dubbed 'lighter'), the letters 'GAZ' inscribed into an ellipse or the Cyrillic letters 'ГАЗ', the A representing a drilling rig with flames on top (hence the nickname 'Gazprom on fire').

Registration	Version	C/n	F/n	Notes
RA-74005	An-74TK-100S	365.470.94.892	1310	Ex-Nadym Air Enterprise/ Nadym Gasprom, bought 1998, full Nadym Gasprom c/s, later full GZP c/s, 'lighter' logo
RA-74008	An-74T-100	365.470.95.900	1405	Converted An-74, ex-Khar'kov State Aircraft Manufacturing Co. UR-74008, bought 1997. Basic Aeroflot polar c/s, later full GZP c/s, 'lighter' logo
RA-74011	*An-74*	*47136013*	*0103P?*	*Khar'kov shipset 1809 Lsf Shar. Inc. 3-96, full Shar c/s and Gazprom titles.*
RA-74012	An-74D	365.470.98.959	1710	Converted An-74-200, ex-Antonov ANTK UR-74055. White overall, Russian flag on tail, no titles
RA-74016	An-74TK-100	365.470.99.1034	2007	Full GZP c/s, 'lighter' logo
RA-74030	*An-74*	*365.470.98.957*	*1709*	*All-white c/s, no titles. Sold to K. S. Avia 2003 as YL-KSA*
RA-74031	An-74-200	365.470.98.961	1802	Bought 1997, ex-RDS-Avia
RA-74032	An-74-200	365.470.98.962	1803	Ex-Vitair UR-74032, bought 1996
RA-74035	An-74-200	365.470.98.963	1804	Ex-Nadym Air Enterprise/ Nadym Gasprom (also reported as Tyumen'transgaz), bought 7-97. Basic Aeroflot colours, no titles
RA-74036	An-74-200	365.470.98.965	1805	Ex-Nadym Air Enterprise/ Nadym Gasprom (also rep. as Tyumen'transgaz), bought 7-97. Full c/s, 'GAZ' logo
RA-74044	An-74-200	365.470.97.936	1607	Bought 1997, ex-Aero Eko UN-74044, ex-RDS-Avia RA-74044. Basic Aeroflot polar c/s
RA-74045	An-74-200	365.470.97.938	1608	Bought 1997, ex-RDS-Avia; stored Ostaf'yevo in basic Aeroflot polar c/s with RDS-Avia titles
RA-74056	An-74-200	365.470.98.951	1706	Ex-Mostransgaz, bought 1995. Full c/s, 'Gazprom on fire' logo. Was leased to Air Afrique (dates unknown)
RA-74058	An-74-200	365.470.98.956	1708	Ex-Mostransgaz, bought 1995. Full c/s, 'Gazprom on fire' logo. Damaged Novyy Urengoy 23-12-95 and repaired
RA-74060	*An-74-200*	*365.470.98.966*	*1806*	*Ex-Tyumen'transgaz, bought 7-97; sold to Tulpar*

• **Klyuch Avia** ('Key Air') based at Samara-Smyshlyayevka was the first operator of the aforementioned An-74 RA-74040, taking delivery in 1993. The real owner of the aircraft was the Samara Metal Foundry.

• **Kolyma Avia [–/KLI]** based in Magadan briefly leased An-74s RA-74009 (formerly Moldova-74009, c/n 365.470.95.898, f/n 1403) from Valeologia Airlines in December 1992/May 1993.

• **Koryak Avia** (the airline of the Koryak Autonomous District) based in Tilichiki on the Kamchatka Peninsula owned two An-74s, RA-74039 (c/n 365.470.97.931, f/n 1603) and RA-74050 (c/n 47181011, f/n 1704/0101P).

• **Kras Air** (Krasnoyarsk Airlines/*Krasno**yar**skiye avia**lin**ii*) **[7B/KJC]** based at Krasnoyarsk-Yemel'yanovo reportedly operated An-74 CCCP-74004 No.2 (later RA-74004, c/n 365.470.94.890, f/n 1309) in 1992-95. The aircraft was transferred to the Noril'sk Air Enterprise.

• **Moscow Airways [M8/MSC]** based at Sheremet'yevo-2 ordered a single An-74 (or probably more) in the early 1990s. The first aircraft, RA-74013 (c/n 47195015, f/n 1902/0105P?) was built in Omsk and was already painted in full Moscow Airways colours when the airline's operating licence was revoked in 1996 due to unsatisfactory operational standards. (The crash of An-32B RA-26222 at Kinshasa-N'dolo on 8th January 1996 when the aircraft ploughed through the adjacent Simba Zikita market, killing some 260 people, was the last straw.) Hence the aircraft was never delivered and the 'unlucky' registration was changed to RA-74017 before the machine went to Polartrans in 2004.

• **Mostransgaz**, one of the natural gas industry's initially independent flying divisions, had two An-74-200s (RA-74056 and RA-74058) until it merged into Gazpromavia in 1997.

• An-74 RA-74027 was briefly operated by **Musa Motors**, the Russian authorised dealer for Volvo and Land Rover cars, in December 1992.

• Three An-74-200s (RA-74005, RA-74035 and RA-74036) were operated by **Nadym Gasprom** (*sic*) in a striking red/blue/white colour scheme. In July 1997 the airline was likewise absorbed by Gazpromavia.

• The fleet of the **Noril'sk Air Enterprise** (*No**ril'**skoye **a**viapred-pri**yah**tiye*), the successor of the Krasnoyarsk CAD/Noril'sk UAD, included An-74 RA-74004.

• **Polyot Russian Airlines** (*Ros**seey**skaya aviakom**pah**niya 'Po**lyot**'*) **[–/POT]** operated An-74 RA-74024 (c/n 365.470.96.918, f/n 1505) in 1992-93. The aircraft was owned by the Staryy Oskol Metal Foundry. In 1993 the machine was sold to Vostsibaero.

• In 1994 the Batagai, Chokurdakh, Kolyma-Indigirka and Tiksi divisions of Sakha Avia (see below) assumed a new identity, becoming **Polar Airlines** (*Po**lyar**nyye avia**lin**ii*). Among other things, the new car-

Registration	Version	C/n	F/n	Notes
RA-74000	*An-74*	*365.470.60.649*	*0609*	*Transferred 21-4-94. Sold to Moldova as ER-AEO*
RA-74001	*An-74TK-100*	*365.470.70.655*	*0701*	*Transferred 21-4-94. Sold to Sakha Aviation Personnel Training Centre by 8-03*

RA-74003	*An-74*	*365.470.70.690*	*0706*	*Transferred 21-4-94. Sold to Sakha Aviation Personnel Training Centre by 8-03*
RA-74006	An-74	365.470.95.896	1402	Transferred 20-7-95

• A trio of An-74-200s registered RA-74031, RA-74044 and RA-74045 was operated by **RDS-Avia**, the flying division of the ***Roos**skiy dom* ***Sel**enga* (Selenga Russian House) trading company. The latter eventually turned out to be a financial pyramid; when the scam was exposed (too late, as usual – that is, when the company bosses had absconded with the clients' money!), all three aircraft were impounded and eventually appropriated by Gazpromavia.

• By far the greatest numbers of An-72s operated by the Soviet Air Force and the Soviet Naval Aviation were stationed in Russia. They became part of the **Russian Air Force** after the break-up of the Soviet Union. Known units operating the type included the 8th ADON at Chkalovskaya AB and the 978th VTAP (*vo**yen**no-**trahns**portnyy* ***a**via-**polk*** – military airlift regiment, ≈ Military Airlift Wing) at Klin-5 AB, Moscow DD. Nearly half of the Russian Air Force's *Coalers* are An-72S 'brass hat haulers'. Today the bulk of these aircraft are mothballed due to spares problems and/or budgetary constraints.

Due to the Soviet/Russian system of tactical codes the c/n is the only positive way of identifying aircraft in overt military markings. Hence, while quasi-civil aircraft are listed in registration order, the ones with tactical codes are listed in c/n order. A few An-72Ps with unknown c/ns are included in the Border Guards section, as duplication is unlikely due to the scarcity of this version. Some Soviet Air Force

Registration/ tactical code	Version	C/n	F/n	Notes
CCCP-72900	An-72	365.720.20.337	0301	
CCCP-72901	An-72	365.720.20.358	0302	
CCCP-72902	An-72	365.720.20.362	0303	
CCCP-72903	An-72	365.720.20.385	0305	
RA-72905	An-72S	365.720.30.430	0402	Based Ostaf'yevo
CCCP-72906	An-72	365.720.30.447	0403	
CCCP-72907	An-72	365.720.20.375	0304	Possibly Siberian DD
RA-72908	An-72S?	365.720.94.880	1303	Blue/white tail
CCCP-72910	An-72	365.720.30.455	0405	
RA-72911	An-72	365.720.30.460	0406	Blue/white tail
RA-72913	An-72	365.720.30.477	0409	Based Chkalovskaya AB
CCCP-72916/ '02 Red'	An-72S?	365.720.40.525	0502	Blue/white tail. Northern Group of Forces? Became, see next line
RA-72916				Blue/white tail
RA-72917	An-72S	365.720.40.530	0503	Blue/white tail. Based Chkalovskaya AB, all-passenger version
RA-72918	An-72	365.720.40.548	0504	Blue/white tail. Based Chkalovskaya AB. Leased or sold to Yamal Airlines by 8-03
RA-72919	An-72	365.720.40.565	0508	Based Chkalovskaya AB
RA-72920	An-72	365.720.40.570	0509	Based Chkalovskaya AB
CCCP-72921	An-72	365.720.40.581	0510	
RA-72922	An-72	365.720.40.560	0506	Based St. Petersburg/Leningrad DD
RA-72924	An-72	365.720.60.600	0602	Based Chkalovskaya AB
RA-72925	An-72	365.720.40.563	0507	Blue/white tail
RA-72926	An-72	365.720.60.620	0604	
CCCP-72927	An-72	365.720.60.625	0605	Blue/white tail
RA-72928	*An-72*	*365.720.60.640*	*0606*	*Sold to Angolan Air Force as T700 by 2001*
RA-72929	*An-72*	*365.720.60.653*	*0610*	*Based Chkalovskaya AB. Sold to Libyan Air Cargo by 2003 as 3C-QTA*
RA-72930	An-72S	365.720.70.678	0702	Blue/white tail, all-passenger version. Based Chkalovskaya AB
CCCP-72931	*An-72S?*	*365.720.70.695*	*0707*	*Blue/white tail. Sold to Enimex 4-95 as ES-NOB*
RA-72934	*An-72*	*365.720.80.777*	*0802*	*Sold to Air Cess ?-98 as 3D-RTV*
RA-72936	*An-72*	*365.720.60.642*	*0607*	*Blue/white tail. 978th VTAP, based Klin-5 AB. Sold to civil operator by 8-03 as An-72-100*
RA-72937	An-72S?	365.720.70.688	0704	Blue/white tail. 978th VTAP, based Klin-5 AB
RA-72938	An-72S	365.720.70.693	0706	Based Chkalovskaya AB.
RA-72939	*An-72S*	*365.720.80.780*	*0804*	*Sold to Enimex 2-97 as An-72-100 ES-NOK*
RA-72940	An-72	365.720.80.781	0805	Based Chkalovskaya AB
CCCP-72941	An-72	365.720.80.783	0806	
RA-72942	*An-72S*	*365.720.80.786*	*0807*	*Based Chkalovskaya AB. Sold to Enimex 9-97 as An-72-100 ES-NOG*
CCCP-72943	An-72	365.720.80.787	0808	Based Chkalovskaya AB?
RA-72944	*An-72*	*365.720.90.796*	*0902*	*Sold to Air Cess ?-98 as 3D-RTW*
RA-72945	An-72	365.720.90.799	0903	
RA-72946	An-72	365.720.90.801	0904	Blue/white tail. Based Chkalovskaya AB?
RA-72947	An-72S?	365.720.90.803	0905	Blue/white tail. Based Chkalovskaya AB
CCCP-72951	An-72	365.720.90.809	0909	Blue/white tail
RA-72952	An-72	365.720.91.823	1004	Based Chkalovskaya AB?
CCCP-72953	An-72	365.720.80.793	0810	
RA-72954	An-72	365.720.90.795	0901	Based Yermolino
RA-72962	An-72	365.720.91.831	1008	
RA-72963	An-72	365.720.92.845	1103	Based Chkalovskaya AB
RA-72967	An-72	365.720.91.837	1010	Based Yermolino
RA-72968	An-72	365.720.92.838	1101	Based Yermolino
CCCP-72969	An-72	365.720.92.848	1105	Based Yermolino
RA-72956	An-72	365.720.92.853	1107	978th VTAP, based Klin-5 AB
CCCP-72957	An-72	365.720.92.856	1108	978th VTAP, based Klin-5 AB
RA-72964	An-72	365.720.93.860	1201	Based Chkalovskaya AB?
RA-72965	An-72	365.720.93.863	1202	
RA-72971	An-72	365.720.93.873	1208	Based Yermolino
CCCP-72975	An-72S	365.720.94.888	1307	To Valeologia as 72975
RA-72979	An-72	365.470.95.908	1409	Based Chkalovskaya AB?
RA-72980	*An-72*	*365.720.95.909*	*1410*	*Sold to Centrafricain Airlines ?-2000 as EL-ALX*
RA-72982	*An-72*	*365.720.96.914*	*1503*	*Sold ?-00 as 3C-QQO*
RA-72991	An-72	365.720.10.949?	0203?	Blue/white tail. Ex-Russian Air Force '11 Red'?
RA-72992	An-72	?	?	
CCCP-783061/ '37 Red'	An-72R	365.720.10.930	0104	Second prototype, operated by GNIKI VVS
CCCP-783573/ '38 Red'	An-72R	365.720.10.935	0105	Third prototype, operated by GNIKI VVS
CCCP-784072/ '39 Red'	An-72R	365.720.10.940	0201	Fourth prototype, operated by GNIKI VVS
'11 Red'	An-72	365.720.10.949	0203	Presumably became RA-72991
no code	*An-72*	*365.720.10.952*	*0204*	*Grey c/s. Sold to Enimex 10-98 and converted to An-72-100 ES-NOC*
'58 Red'	An-72	365.720.30.468	0407	
'24'?	*An-72*	*365.720.60.610*	*0603*	*Tactical code unconfirmed. Transferred to LII as '03 Red'*

Above: An-74TK-100S RA-74005 (c/n 365.470.94.892, f/n 1310) in full Gazpromavia livery is shown in the static park of the Civil Aviation-2002 show at Moscow-Domodedovo on 15th August 2002. The red '*Vozdooshnaya skoraya pomoshch*' (Air Ambulance) titles had been applied that very day.

Another view of An-74TK-100S RA-74005 at Moscow-Domodedovo, with a makeshift beer restaurant as a backdrop. As an aside, the event was a real feast for spotters, as the show was running right in the midst of an operating airport, with lots of aircraft movements, and beer and other goodies readily available.

Above: An-74-200 RA-74036 (c/n 365.470.998.965, f/n 1805) represents a variation on the usual standard, featuring a 'GAZ' tail logo instead of the usual 'lighter' and grey (not blue) undersides. The cheatline is also slightly different.

An-74-200 RA-74060 (c/n 365.470.98.966, f/n 1806) is seen here on the cargo (west) apron at Moscow-Domodedovo shortly after repainting in Koopol-Avia's striking colour scheme. Earlier it had worn basic Tulpar colours.

Above: An-72 CCCP-72925 (c/n 365.720.40.563, f/n 0507) is one of many Soviet/Russian Air Force examples sporting blue/white tails. This version of the Aeroflot livery certainly looks more appealing than the white-tail standard.

An-72S CCCP-72916/'02 Red' (c/n 365.720.40.525, f/n 0502) is seen here visiting Akhtoobinsk, with a Sukhoi Su-27 and several Mikoyan MiG-31s in the background. Note the welded steel jet blast deflectors for the fighters at the edge of the hardstand.

Above: Russian Air Force An-72S '01 Red' used to be quasi-civil; a close look reveals the overpainted Soviet flag on the fin and overpainted Aeroflot titles/logo on the nose. Its previous identity is unknown.

Another view of '01 Red'.

Above: In contrast, the previous identity of some red-starred An-72s is obvious. '948 Black' seen here at its home base, Chkalovskaya AB, is ex-CCCP-72948 (c/n 365.720.91.815, f/n 1001). Note the higher position of the star on the white tail and the canvas covers on the wings.

A fine landing study of An-72 CCCP-72908 (c/n 365.720.94.880, f/n 1303). Note that the APU is running.

'1'	An-72	365.720.70.770	0710	
'2'	An-72	365.720.90.805	0906	
'23'	An-72	365.720.90.810	0910	
'948 Black'	An-72	365.720.91.815	1001	Ex-CCCP-72948, basic Aeroflot c/s
'949 Black'	An-72S	365.720.91.818	1002	Ex-CCCP-72949, basic Aeroflot c/s
'950 Black'	An-72	365.720.91.819	1003	Ex-CCCP-72950, basic Aeroflot c/s
'21'	An-72	365.720.93.868	1205	
'70 Red'	An-72	365.720.93.872	1207	Based Yermolino
'09 Blue'	An-72	365.720.93.875	1209	Grey c/s
'33'	*An-72*	*365.720.93.876*	*1210*	*To Tiramavia as ER-AWS*
'976 Black'	An-72	365.720.94.884	1305	Ex-CCCP-72976, basic Aeroflot c/s

Some of the Russian Air Force's An-72s have been retrofitted with lateral chaff/flare dispensers for self-protection during overhauls. The quasi-civil examples usually wore standard Aeroflot livery, and still do; many of them have blue/white tails.

• A few An-72s (mainly VIP transports) were operated by **the Soviet/Russian Naval Air Arm**. Known examples are An-72 RA-72914 (c/n 365.720.30.479, f/n 0410) and An-72S RA-72974 (c/n 365.720.94.878, f/n 1302) based at Moscow-Ostaf'yevo.

• A number of An-72s was operated by the aviation component of the KGB's Border Guards. In post-Soviet times this was transformed into the **Federal Border Guards** as an organisationally separate arm; this was merged back into the FSB (Federal Security Service, the KGB's successor) in 2004.

Registration/ tactical code	Version	C/n	F/n	Notes
RA-72909	An-72	365.720.40.550	0505	
CCCP-72923	An-72S?	365.720.60.590	0601	Blue/white tail. KGB Border Guards; based Leningrad-Pulkovo?
RA-72958	An-72	365.720.92.841	1102	FBG, based Moscow/Sheremet'yevo-1
RA-72960	An-72S	365.720.93.865	1203	FBG, based Moscow/Sheremet'yevo-1. DBR Vorkuta 23-10-94
RA-72961	An-72S	365.720.93.866	1204	FBG, based Moscow/Sheremet'yevo-1
CCCP-72970	An-72P	365.760.93.870	1206	Basic Aeroflot c/s, based Yuzhno-Sakhalinsk
'04 Blue'	An-72P	365.760.90.808?	0908?	FBG, camouflaged
'22 Blue'	An-72P	365.760.91.825?	1005?	FBG, camouflaged, based Petropavlovsk-Kamchatskiy
'26'	An-72P	365.760.91.827	1006	
'24 Blue'	An-72P	365.760.91.830?	1007?	Ex-'22'? FBG, camouflaged, based Petropavlovsk-Kamchatskiy
'01 Red'	An-72P	365.760.92.850	1106	Basic AFL c/s, star insignia on tail
'2'	An-72P	365.760.92.859	1110	
'58 Blue'	An-72P	365.760.94.885	1306	Basic Aeroflot c/s, Russian flag on tail; based Yuzhno-Sakhalinsk
'2'	An-72P	365.760.95.899	1404	
'03 Red'	An-72P	?	?	Basic AFL c/s, star insignia on tail
'22 Red'	An-72P	?	?	Basic AFL c/s, Russian flag on tail
'27 Blue'	An-72P	?	?	
'35 Blue'	An-72	?	?	978th VTAP, Klin-5 AB
'59 Yellow'	An-72P	?	?	

• The **Russian Ministry of Emergency Control (EMERCOM) [–/SUM]** responsible for rescue and relief operations during natural disasters and major accidents has a large paramilitary force at its disposal. Personnel, equipment and humanitarian cargoes are transported by a sizeable fleet of aircraft, including two An-74Ps – RA-74029 (c/n 365.470.97.940, f/n 1609) and RA-74034 (c/n 47136012, f/n 1707/0102P); both are based at Zhukovskiy.

Originally RA-74029 wore basic Aeroflot polar colours modified by adding a 'lightning bolt' cheatline and EMERCOM insignia. The other aircraft had a totally different colour scheme from the start, with a kinked orange/blue/orange cheatline and the familiar roundel markings incorporated into a windrose. In 1998 most of EMERCOM's fleet was christened; like most aircraft, the An-74s are named after famous Soviet pilots, including the first Heroes of the Soviet Union. Thus, RA-74029 is named *Gheorgiy Baidukov* and RA-74034 is *Aleksandr Belyakov* – the two other crewmen who flew with Valeriy Chkalov on his record-setting non-stop cross-Polar flight to the USA.

• **Sakha Avia [K7/IKT]**, originally called **Yakutavia**, was the national airline of the Republic of Yakutia (Sakha) and one of the biggest Russian air carriers. It was headquartered in Yakutsk, comprising several branches (air enterprises); the fixed-wing fleet included four An-74s in basic red/white Aeroflot polar colours.

Registration	Version	C/n	F/n	Notes
RA-74000	An-74	365.470.60.649	0609	Kolyma-Indigirka Air Enterprise. Transferred to Polar Airlines 21-4-94
RA-74001	An-74TK-100	365.470.70.655	0701	Converted An-74. Cherskiy AE, later to Kolyma-Indigirka AE. Transferred to Polar Airlines 21-4-94
RA-74003	An-74	365.470.70.690	0706	Cherskiy AE, later to Kolyma-Indigirka AE. Transferred to Polar Airlines 21-4-94
RA-74006	An-74	365.470.95.896	1402	Kolyma-Indigirka AE. Transferred to Polar Airlines 20-7-95

In the late 1990s Sakha Avia suffered from excess capacity and much of its enormous fleet was put in storage or disposed of. The airline ceased operations in 2003, breaking up into several smaller carriers. In 2002 the An-74s listed above were noted with '*Respooblika Sakha*' titles, but it is not clear whether they had been returned to Sakha Avia.

• The **Sakha Aviation Personnel Training Centre** (*Sakha tsentr podgotovki aviatsionnovo personahla*), also located in Yakutsk, took over An-74s RA-74001 and RA-74003 after the demise of Sakha-Avia.

• The **2nd Sverdlovsk Air Enterprise** (*Vtoroye Sverdlovskoye aviapredpriyahtiye*) based at Yekaterinburg-Uktus operates An-74D RA-74048 leased from Bashkirian Airlines in 2002. The aircraft is all-white without titles.

• **Severgazprom**, another natural gas industry flying division based in the city of Ukhta (Komi Autonomous Republic), leased An-74T-100 RA-74008 from the Khar'kov State Aircraft Manufacturing Co. in 1995.

• **Shar, Inc. [–/UGP]**, a subsidiary of the Koopol Electromechanical Plant (a defence industry enterprise), operated up to ten An-72/An-74s from Moscow-Ostaf'yevo.

Because of the parent company's name two of the aircraft, RA-74024 and RA-74060, were operated with **Koopol-Avia** titles and logos after 2000. The former aircraft sported a stylish livery with a white belly and a two-tone blue top, while RA-74060 was in basic Tulpar colours. RA-74024 is now reportedly operated jointly with the **Mikhail V. Khrunichev Space Centre** (an enterprise manufacturing, among other things, Proton space launch vehicles) and wears 'Proton' titles.

Above: The Russian Federal Border Guards (now part of the Federal Security Service) were the largest operator of the armed An-72P. '01 Red' (c/n 365.760.92.850, f/n 1106) is one of several examples in basic Aeroflot colours with 'Ан-72П' nose titles; it is shown here in seldom seen gunless configuration.

'03 Red', another red-starred An-72P in basic Aeroflot colours (c/n unknown); the star insignia on the tail are smaller than on unarmed Air Force examples (cf. '948 Black' on page 110). The shadow on the fin shows clearly the deployed deflectors on the stabiliser leading edges.

Above: Showing off its fairly fresh camouflage colours, Russian Federal Border Guards An-72P '04 Blue' (presumably c/n 365.760.90.808, f/n 0908) comes in to land at Moscow-Sheremet'yevo.

As this view of '04 Blue' shows, the red FBG identification stripes are applied not only to the rudder but to the elevators (spanwise) as well.

Above: An-74 RA-74034 (c/n 47136012, f/n 1707/0102P) in new EMERCOM of Russia colours with the orange/blue/orange cheatline sits on a snow-covered ramp at Moscow-Bykovo on 17th March 1996. The aircraft was still nameless then. Note the red horizontal tail and the red outer wings.

Ex-Aviacor RA-74041, the sole An-74-200 operated by Sibaviatrans (c/n 365.470.96.924, f/n 1509), is shown here at its home base of Krasnoyarsk-Yemel'yanovo.

Registration	Version	C/n	F/n	Notes
RA-72905	An-72S	365.720.30.430	0402	Leased from Russian Naval Air Arm
RA-74001	*An-74TK-100*	*365.470.70.655*	*0701*	*Converted An-74. leased from Cherskiy Air Enterprise*
RA-74011	*An-74*	*47136013*	*0103P?*	*Khar'kov shipset 1809. Full c/s, was leased to Gazpromavia. Sold to Kazakhstan 6-99 as UN 74011*
RA-74015	An-74	365.470.98.969	1808	Leased from Bashkirian Airlines ?-03
RA-74024	An-74	365.470.96.918	1505	
RA-74040	*An-74*	*365.470.97.930*	*1602*	*Leased from United Energy Systems of Russia/Aviaenergo*
RA-74041	An-74-200	365.470.96.924	1509	Leased from Sibaviatrans ?-02
RA-74052	*An-74-200*	*365.470.98.944*	*1702*	*Basic Aeroflot polar c/s. Sold to Yamal Airlines*
RA-74060	An-74-200	365.470.98.966	1806	Ex-Tulpar, bought ?-00
ES-NOH	An-72	365.720.95.909	1410	Leased from Enimex 6-02

• The airline **Shonkar** (Falcon in Bashkirian) based in Ufa operated four An-74s (RA-74014, RA-74015, RA-74046 and RA-74047) until it succumbed to to financial problems in 1997 and was absorbed by Bashkirian Airlines.

• **Sibaviatrans** (aka **SIAT**) **[5M/SIB]** incorporated on 1st February 1995 as the flying division of the Krasnoyarsk Metal Foundry and based at Krasnoyarsk-Yemel'yanovo operated a single An-74-200, RA-74041, bought from Aviacor in 1996. The aircraft, which is in ten-seat combi configuration, wears the airline's attractive livery with red and blue trim and is on lease to Shar, Inc. since 2002.

• **Severgazprom** (North Gas Industry), another natural gas industry flying division based in Ukhta (Komi Autonomous Republic), leased An-74T-100 RA-74008 from the Khar'kov State Aircraft Manufacturing Co. in 1995.

• The flying division of **TsSKB Progress [–/PSS]** (*Tsentrahl'noye spetsiahl'noye konstrooktorskoye byuro* – Central Special Design Bureau) based at the industrial airfield of Samara-Bezymyanka operated An-72-100D RA-72982 in basic Aeroflot colours. TsSKB Progress is an enterprise which created, among other things, the aforementioned Proton SLV. The aircraft was sold to San Air (supposedly a Kyrghyz airline) in 2001 as 3C-QQO!

• Kazan'-based **Tulpar [–/TUL]** (the name means 'winged steed' in Tatarian) bought An-74-200 UR-74055 (c/n 365.470.98.959, f/n 1710) in 1996. Reregistered RA-74012, the aircraft was operated initially with an Aeroflot cheatline and then in all-white colours until it was sold to Gazpromavia in 1999 and became an An-74D. Judging by its colour scheme, An-74-200 RA-74060 also served with Tulpar for a while until likewise sold to Gazpromavia; however, it may be that it was ordered by Tulpar but never delivered.

• The small fleet of the Irkutsk-based charter carrier **Vostsibaero** (East Siberian Airlines) included two An-74-200s, RA-74024 and RA-74037 (c/n 365.470.98.950, f/n 1705). Unfortunately the latter aircraft crashed on take-off at Mirnyy on 10th December 1999 and the ensuing investigation ended in the airline's licence being withdrawn.

• **Yamal Airlines [YL/LLM]** based in Salekhard on the Yamal Peninsula in the Russian High North has three An-74s in full livery; the fleet was augmented lately by a single An-72 in basic Aeroflot colours. All four aircraft are leased out to Alliance-Avia.

Registration	Version	C/n	F/n	Notes
RA-72918	An-72	365.720.40.548	0504	Bought or leased from the Russian Air Force; (sub-) leased to Alliance-Avia by 8-03. Basic Aeroflot c/s, blue/white tail
RA-74027	An-74-200	365.470.96.920	1507	Ex-Ukraine Air Alliance UR-74027, full c/s. Leased from Alliance-Avia ?-00
RA-74043	An-74-200	365.470.96.923	1508	Ex-Ukraine Air Alliance UR-74043, full c/s. Leased from Alliance-Avia 1-12-00 to 1-12-03
RA-74052	An-74-200	365.470.98.944	1702	Ex-Shar, Inc. Full c/s. Leased from Alliance-Avia ?-01

GEORGIA

• A single Georgian-registered An-72, 4L-AAP (c/n unknown), made its appearance in April 2003. Originally flown without any titles or logos, it gained the insignia of **Air Van** in January 2004.

• Later that year 4L-AAP was seen wearing the insignia of a company called **IAP**.

KAZAKSTAN

• The Kazakh airline **Aero-Eko** leased two An-74-200s, RA-74044 (c/n 365.470.97.936, f/n 1607) and RA-74045 (c/n 365.470.97.938, f/n1608) from Moscow-based RDS-Avia in 1995-96. Both machines were placed on the Kazakh register as UN-74044 and UN-74045, regaining their Russian identities after the lease expired. A third example, UN-74031, was bought from Vitair (ex-UR-74031, c/n 365.470.98.961, f/n 1802); it was sold to Aeroservice Cargo in June 1996.

• **Aeroservice Cargo** operated An-74-200 UN-74031 for just over a year before selling it to RDS-Avia in November 1997 as RA-74031.

• An **unidentified Kazakh airline** purchased An-74 RA-74011 (c/n 47136013, f/n 1809/0103P) from Gazpromavia in June 1999 and the aircraft was reregistered UN 74011. The machine was sold to the Ukrainian carrier Khoriv Avia in 2003 as UR-CAC.

• The **Kazakstan Air Force** operated a number of An-72s. The aircraft belonged to the composite special mission air squadron stationed in Almaty.

Registration/ tactical code	Version	C/n	F/n	Notes
UN-72904	An-72	365.720.30.425	0401	Became, see next line
72904	An-72			UN- country prefix removed by 2001
'01 Red'	An-72	365.720.30.470	0408	
'02 Red'	An-72P	?	?	

KYRGHYZSTAN

In 2001 An-72-100D RA-72982 was cancelled from the Russian register as leased to Kyrghyzstan. Soon the machine surfaced under the operator name **San Air**; the name is in no way connected with SAN [S3/SND], a Kazakh-German joint venture based in Karaganda, which had ceased operations by then. For some obscure reason the aircraft was registered in Equatorial Guinea (!) as 3C-QQO. In 2004 the jet was sold to Enimex, which promptly leased it to Atlantic Airlines.

MOLDOVA (MOLDAVIA)

• Valeologia Airlines, one of the first post-Aeroflot airlines established in Moldova, started operations with three *Coalers* in 1992. The first two were former Soviet Air Force aircraft.

Registration	Version	C/n	F/n	Notes
CCCP-72975	An-72S	365.720.94.888	1307	CCCP- prefix later deleted. Leased to Natar ?-95; sold to Renan 12-95 as ER-ACF
CCCP-72977	An-72S	365.720.94.889	1308	Leased to Helitaxi Colombia as HK-3808X 12-92 to 5-93; returned as, ER-72977 Leased to Natar ?-95; sold to to Renan 12-95 as ER-ACA
Moldova-74009	An-74	365.470.95.898	1403	Leased to Kolyma Avia as RA-74009 12-92 to 5-93. Sold to Renan 2-95 as ER-ACN

• The three aircraft listed above served with **Renan [–/RAN]**, a Kishinyov-based cargo airline, for several more years. An-72 ER-ACF had an unlucky fate: on 22nd December 1997 it went missing over the Atlantic Ocean off the coast of Angola –, and the fake registration ER-AER was entered into the Moldovan state civil aircraft register to cover up the loss.

Sister ship ER-ACA was reregistered ER-AEJ for some reason in 1996 and sold or leased to an obscure airline called Shemair in 2003, while An-74 ER-ACN was similarly reregistered ER-AEN.

• **Air Moldova [9U/MLD]**, the national flag carrier, briefly operated An-74 ER-ACN from Kishinyov (Chisinau) in 1996 on lease from Renan.

• The **Moldovan Air Force** (FARM – *Fortele Aeriene de Republica Moldova*) took over a pair of white-tailed An-72s registered CCCP-72932 (c/n 365.720.70.696, f/n 0708) and CCCP-72933 (c/n 365.720.70.698, f/n 0709). Reregistered ER-72932 and ER-72933, the aircraft were based at Kishinyov and used in support of the Moldovan MoD top brass. This included occasional participation in international military exercises, such as *Co-operative Bear '96*.

• In 2001 both aircraft were transferred to **Vichi Airlines [–/VIH]**, the commercial division of FARM, receiving the new registrations ER-AWF and ER-AFZ respectively. The jets wore a grey/white colour scheme without titles. In 2003 ER-AFZ briefly regained its former registration (with no prefix, as 72933) but then reverted to Vichi as ER-AWF.

• **Tiramavia [–/TVI]**, the flying division of an electronics industry enterprise (formerly known as Mikma [–/ITL]), operated a single An-72 registered ER-AWS (ex-Russian Air Force '33', c/n 365.720.93.876, f/n 1210) in 2003. In 2004 the jet was sold to the Angolan Air Force and serialled T-702.

THE UKRAINE

• **Air Ukraine/Avialinii Ukraïny [6U/UKR]**, the Ukrainian flag carrier, operated a single An-72 (UR-72959) leased from the Ukrainian Air Force in the mid-1990s. The aircraft wore the airline's fleetwide standard livery introduced in late 1993 – that is, predominantly white with a yellow rear fuselage and a blue tail carrying Air Ukraine's tail logo (a stylised blue bird on a yellow circle).

• The **Antonov Design Bureau** operates a large fleet of assorted aircraft of its own make, including An-72s and An-74s.

Registration/ tactical code	Version	C/n	F/n	Notes
CCCP-71052	*An-72*	*365.720.80.775*	*0801*	*Overall grey c/s; avionics testbed?*
CCCP-72000	An-72	005	–	Ex-CCCP-19795, second prototype. WFU Kiev-Gostomel'?
CCCP-72002	*An-72*	*365.720.10.9...?*	*0205?*	
CCCP-72003	An-74	003	–	Ex-CCCP-780334, prototype. WFU Kiev-Gostomel'
72966	An-72G	365.720.92.847	1104	WFU Kiev-Gostomel' after mid-air collision with first prototype An-70
UR-74008	*An-74*	*365.470.95.900*	*1405*	*Basic Aeroflot polar c/s. Sold to Severgazprom as An-74T-100 RA-74008*
UR-74010	An-74T	365.470.30.450	0404	Prototype, basic Aeroflot blue/white c/s; later converted to VIP aircraft, full Antonov Airlines c/s
UR-74027	*An-74-200*	*365.470.96.920*	*1507*	*Ex-Musa Motors RA-74027; sold to Vitair in 1995*
UR-74028	An-74	365.720.10.947	0202	Ex-CCCP-58642, first production An-74. DBR (date unknown) and WFU Kiev-Gostomel'
UR-74055	*An-74*	*365.470.98.959*	*1710*	*White overall, no titles. Sold to Gazpromavia as An-74D RA-74012*
CCCP-780151	An-71	01	–	First prototype, converted from An-72 CCCP-72004 No 1 c/n 004. WFU Kiev-Gostomel'
CCCP-780361	An-71	03	–	Second prototype. WFU Kiev-Svyatoshino
'06 Yellow'	An-72P	006	–	Prototype; modified with IAI mission avionics, later reconverted
'11 Red'	*An-72*	*365.720.10.905*	*0101*	*Ukrainian Air Force markings. Sold to Enimex as ES-NOP 7-01*
no code	An-72R	365.720.10.912?	0103?	First prototype, WFU Kiev-Svyatoshino

• **CABI Airlines [–/CBI]** (the acronym means 'Connection, aviation, business, information') operated a single An-74 registered UR-74057 (c/n 365.470.98.960, f/n 1801) in 1997-2001.

• The **Khar'kov State Aircraft Manufacturing Co. (KSAMC) [–/WKH]** ran a small fleet of aircraft, including its own product – the An-74 in its various forms.

Registration/ tactical code	Version	C/n	F/n	Notes
CCCP-74007	An-74	365.470.95.903	1406	Leased to Helitaxi Colombia as HK-3808-X 12-92 to 5-93; returned as, see next line.
UR-74007				Leased to Aero Charter 1-03
CCCP-74008	*An-74*	*365.470.95.900*	*1405*	*Converted to, see next line*
UR-74008	*An-74T-100*			*Sold to Gazpromavia as RA-74008*
UR-74038	An-74TK-200	365.470.97.933	1605	Demonstrator aircraft
UR-74300	An-74TK-300	365.470.98.984	1910	Prototype. Leased to Ukraine Air Enterprise as UR-LDK

• Kiev/Zhulyany-based **Khoriv Avia [–/KRV]**, a commercial division of the Ukrainian MoD, operated two An-74s – UR-BYH (c/n 365.470.98.946, f/n 1703) and UR-CAC (c/n 47136013, f/n 1809/0103P). The latter aircraft was sold to K.S. Avia of Latvia as YL-KSB in 2004, while UR-BYH gained full military markings as '01 Blue'.

(Khoriv was the the name of one of the founders of Kiev in pre-Christian times).

• **Motor-Sich [M9/MSI]**, the flying division of the Zaporozhye-based aero engine factory of the same name, operates An-74T-200 UR-74026 (c/n 365.470.96.919, f/n 1506) which it frequently leases to other carriers.

• The Khar'kov plant likewise leased its aircraft to domestic and Russian carriers on numerous occasions. Among other things, UR-74007 was leased to an organisation called **NARO** in November 1993, the lease continuing to April 1997.

• **Ukraine Air Alliance** (*Ookrayina-Aeroal'yans*) **[–/UKL]** bought both An-74-200s operated by Vitair – UR-74027 (c/n 365.470.96.920, f/n 1507) and UR-74043 (c/n 365.470.96.923, f/n 1508) in 1998. Apparently neither aircraft wore Ukraine Air Alliance titles visibly. Both machines were sold to Yamal Airlines in 1999 and mid-2000 respectively, gaining Russian registrations.

• The **Ukrainian Air Force** (UAF, or VPS – *Voyenno-povitryany seely*) had at least 13 An-72s on strength.

Registration/ tactical code	Version	C/n	F/n	Notes
UR-72959	An-72	365.720.92.858	1109	Based Kiev-Borispol' (16th OSAP?). Was leased to Air Ukraine; became 72959 upon return from the lease
UR-72984	An-72P	365.760.96.926	1510	Based Odessa. UR- prefix later deleted
72985	An-72	365.720.98.973	1901	Reported as an An-72P c/n 365.760.98.973!
UR-74033	An-74	?	?	Grey/white c/s, no titles
'02 Red' (a)	An-72	365.720.60.645	0608	UAF State Flight Research Centre, special white/blue/yellow c/s
'07 Red'	An-72P	365.760.96.915	1504	Basic AFL c/s. Ex-Soviet Air Force '22'
'14 Blue'	An-72P	365.760.97.927	1601	Basic Aeroflot c/s
'01 Blue'	An-74	365.470.98.946	1703	Ex-Khoriv Avia UR-BYH
'02 Red' (b)	An-72	?	?	
'002 Black'	An-72	?	?	Based Kiev-Borispol'; probably became, see next line
'02 Black'				
'07 Red'	An-72	?	?	Based Kiev-Borispol'
'15 Blue'	An-72	?	?	Based Kiev-Borispol'
'59 Red'	An-72P	?	?	

• The **Ukrainian Border Police** operated a single An-74, UR-74053 (c/n 365.470.98.946, f/n 1703), in 1994-98.

• The **Ukrainian Department of Agriculture** operated An-74 UR-74042 (c/n 365.470.97.932, f/n 1604) in 1993-94. The aircraft was sold to Enimex in 1994 as ES-NOE.

• The **Ukrainian government flight** based at Kiev-Borispol' and known since 1996 as the Ukraine Air Enterprise [–/UKN] leased the An-74TK-300 prototype from the Khar'kov State Aircraft Manufacturing Co. in 2003. Since the aircraft was already outfitted with an executive interior, all the new operator had to do was to have the machine repainted in an all-white colour scheme with a thin yellow/blue cheatline, УКРАЇНА (the Ukraine) titles and the national coat of arms on the fuselage.

At first the jet retained its original custom registration UR-74300. Later it received the even more eloquent registration UR-LDK, the last three letters obviously denoting President Leonid Danilovich Kuchma! On reflection, this was not a very good idea, since Kuchma was then in the closing year of his second and final term of office, which meant the aircraft would have to be reregistered after the 2004 Presidential elections, no matter who won.

• Kiev-based **Vitair [–/VIT]** operated five An-74s.

Registration	Version	C/n	F/n	Notes
UR-74008	An-74	365.470.95.900	1405	Leased from KSAMC 1995
UR-74027	*An-74-200*	*365.470.96.920*	*1507*	*Ex-Antonov Design Bureau, bought in 1995; sold to Ukraine Air Alliance*
UR-74031	*An-74-200*	*365.470.98.961*	*1802*	*Sold to Aero Eko 1995 as UN-74031*
UR-74032	*An-74-200*	*365.470.98.962*	*1803*	*Sold to Gazpromavia in 1996 as RA-74032*
UR-74043	*An-74-200*	*365.470.96.923*	*1508*	*Sold to Ukraine Air Alliance*

• An unidentified Ukrainian airline briefly operated An-74-200 UR-74044 (c/n 365.470.97.936, f/n 1607) in basic Aeroflot red/white colours with a Ukrainian flag on the nose and a blue tail logo depicting a stylised crane with the wings raised but no titles. It is not known if the aircraft wore these markings before or after being registered UN 74044 (or RA-74044).

UZBEKISTAN

The national flag carrier **Uzbekistan Airways (Uzbekiston Havo Yullari) [HY/UZB]** briefly leased An-72G 72966 (c/n 365.720.92.847, f/n 1104) from the Antonov Design Bureau in 1994.

The twinjets abroad

A number of An-72s and An-74s have been sold abroad – both as new and used aircraft. In addition to export sales, the *Coaler* has been operated by several airlines outside the CIS on a wet-lease basis.

ANGOLA

• The **Angolan Air Force** (FAA – Força Aérea Angolana) acquired six An-72/An-74s on the second-hand aircraft market, starting in 1977. Some of the aircraft wear overt military markings and are serialled in the T series to denote 'transport'; others ostensibly wear civil registrations but are reported as operated by the Government – and that certainly spells 'm-i-l-i-t-a-r-y'.

Registration/ serial	Version	C/n	F/n	Notes
T-700	An-72	365.470.60.640	0606	Ex-Russian Air Force RA-72928, purchased by 2001; reported as An-74 c/n 365.720.60.640
T-701	An-72V	365.470.95.907	1408	Ex-S9-BOU, ex-Peruvian Air Force OB-1485
T-702	An-72	365.720.93.876	1210	Ex-Tiramavia ER-AWS
T-750	An-72	?	?	
D2-FEP	An-72	?	?	
D2-MBF	An-72	?	?	

• The Luanda-based cargo and passenger carrier **Transaérea, Lda.** leased An-74 RA-74040 from Aviaenergo in 1997 or 1998. The aircraft was returned to the lessor before November 1998.

Above: An-72 '02 Red' (c/n 365.720.60.645, f/n 0608) is operated by the Ukrainian Air Force's State Flight Research Centre in this spectacular colour scheme. It is seen here at RAF Fairford during one of the Royal International Air Tattoos in which it participated more than once. The titles on the other side are in English.

An-74-200 was briefly operated by an unidentified Ukrainian airline in this anonymous colour scheme.

Above: The Ukrainian Border Police also operate a number of An-72Ps, including '14 Blue' (c/n 365.760.97.927, f/n 1601) in basic Aeroflot colours.

Another Ukrainian An-72P '07 Red' (c/n 365.760.96.915, f/n 1504), in fully armed configuration. It was this aircraft that made the An-72P's world debut at Farnborough International '92. Note the red Border Police identification stripe and the tiger badge on the fuselage; the badge was applied for the FI'92 appearance.

BOSNIA-HERZEGOVINA

The Bosnia-Herzegovenian cargo airline **BIO Air Company [–/BIO]**, a division of the Bosnian Investment Organisation, purchased An-74 ES-NOE (c/n 365.470.97.932, f/n 1604) from Enimex in July 1998. The aircraft operated in Estonian markings for almost a year before being reregistered T9-ABE.

BULGARIA

Sofia-based **Scorpion Air [–/SPN]** (also rendered as **Air Scorpio**) leased An-74 UR-74053 (c/n 365.470.98.946, f/n 1703) from the Ukrainian Border Police in 1998, the aircraft changing its identity to LZ-MNM. Just a year later the machine was sold back to the Ukraine, this time to Khoriv-Avia, to become UR-BYH.

COLOMBIA

In December 1992 **Helitaxi Colombia** (which, as the name suggests, is primarily a helicopter operator) leased three Antonov twinjets in the CIS. All three aircraft returned home on 19th May 1993.

Registration	Version	C/n	F/n	Notes
HK-3808-X	An-72	365.720.94.889	1308	Leased from Valeologia, ex CCCP-72977/to ER-ACA; had 'An-74' nose titles!
HK-3809-X	An-74	365.470.95.903	1406	Leased from Khar'kov State Aircraft Manufacturing Co., ex-CCCP-74007/to UR-74007
HK-3810-X	An-74T-200	365.470.96.919	1506	Leased from Motor-Sich, ex-CCCP-74026/to UR-74026

CENTRAL AFRICAN REPUBLIC

Centrafricain Airlines [GC/CET] established in 1998 took over almost the entire fleet of the defunct Air Pass (see Swaziland section), including the two An-72s – TL-ACV (ex-3D-RTV, c/n 365.720.80.777, f/n 0802) and TL-ACW (ex-3D-RTW, c/n 365.720.90.796, f/n 0902). The aircraft were white overall without titles. A third example joined the fleet in late 1999; it was TL-ABC (reportedly ex-RA-72980, c/n 365.720.95.909, f/n 1410), which was later placed on the Liberian register as EL-ALX while still remaining with Centrafricain Airlines. (TL-ABC is unconfirmed as being ex-RA-72980, but EL-ALX is confirmed as being ex-RA-72980.)

Soon these An-72s and several other Soviet-built aircraft became involved in a scandal; it turned out they had been illegally entered into the Central African Republic register. By the way, Centrafricain Airlines, Air Pass (Swaziland) and Air Pass (Liberia) have all been linked with one Victor Bout, a fellow of Russian origins who was notorious as a gun-runner. Obviously when things got too hot the airline would be uprooted and reincarnated in a different place under a different name.

The three aircraft had different fates. EL-ALX was the luckiest of the lot, being sold to Enimex in 2002 to become ES-NOH. TL-ACW, in contrast, was the unluckiest – it was written off in a crash landing at Luzambe, Angola, on 6th October 2000. TL-ACV simply fell into dereliction at Ras al Khaimah, UAE.

EGYPT

The **Egyptian government** has ordered a batch of nine An-74T-200As from the Khar'kov State Aircraft Manufacturing Co. The first aircraft to be delivered (c/n 365.470.98.977, f/n 1904) wore the test registration UR-CES. Judging by the lower rudder segment painted in camouflage colours (the rest of the airframe was finished in grey primer), the aircraft is intended for the **Egyptian Air Force** (*al Quwwat al-Jawwiya il-Misriya*). No Egyptian registration or EAF serial is known yet.

ESTONIA

The Tallinn-based cargo carrier **Enimex [–/ENI]** operated nine An-72s bought from the Russian and Ukrainian air arms. They were initially operated in basic Aeroflot colours with Enimex titles and 'E' tail logo before gaining the full three-tone blue/white livery.

Registration	Version	C/n	F/n	Notes
ES-NOB	An-72-100	365.720.70.695	0707	Ex-Soviet Air Force CCCP-72931, bought 4-95; operated for United Nations, all-white, coded 'UNO-215'
ES-NOC	An-72-100	365.720.10.952	0204	Ex-Soviet Air Force (no code), lsf Antonov ANTK 10-98
ES-NOE		*365.470.97.932*	*1604*	*Ex-UR-74042, sold to BIO Air as T9-ABE*
ES-NOG	An-72-100	365.720.80.786	0807	Ex-Russian Air Force An-72S RA-72942, bought 9-97; operated for United Nations, all-white, coded 'UNO-211'
ES-NOH	An-72-100	365.720.95.909	1410	Ex-EL-ALX, bought and leased to Shar, Inc., 6-02
ES-NOI	An-72-100D	365.720.96.914	1503	Ex-San Air 3C-QQO, ex-Russian Air Force An-72S RA-72982; leased to Atlantic Airlines 10-5-04
ES-NOK	An-72-100	365.720.80.780	0804	Ex-Russian Air Force An-72S RA-72939, bought 2-97; operated for United Nations, all-white, coded 'UN-090'
ES-NOL	An-72	365.720.80.789	0809	Ex-CCCP-72004 No 2, bought ?-96. Sold to Sin Said Airlines as EL-ALL
ES-NOP	*An-72*	*365.720.10.905*	*0101*	*Ex-Ukrainian Air Force '11 Red', bought 7-01. Crash-landed 21-4-02 Wamena, Papua New Guinea, and DBR*

INDONESIA

Mandala Airlines [RI/MDL] based in Jakarta wet-leased An-74T-200 UR-74026 from Motor-Sich in May-June 1997.

IRAN

Starting in 1997, the Iranian Revolutionary Guard took delivery of twelve brand-new An-74s built in Khar'kov; these are the newest examples identified to date. Operating from Teheran-Mehrabad airport, the aircraft mostly wear sand/brown camouflage, although some are painted a nondescript overall dirty white colour.

Serial	Version	C/n	F/n	Notes
15-2250	An-74T-200	365.470.99.1021	2004	
15-2251	An-74	365.470.99.1028	2005	
15-2252	An-74	365.470.99.1032	2006	
15-2253	An-74	365.470.99.1038	2008	
15-2254	An-74T-200	365.470.99.1040	2009	
15-2255	An-74T-200	365.470.99.1045	2010	
15-2256	An-74T-200	365.470.121.1048	2101	White c/s
15-2257	An-74	365.470.121.1050	2102	

Above: An-72-100 ES-NOB (ex-Soviet Air Force CCCP-72931, c/n 365.720.70.695, f/n 0707) displays the full livery of Estonian cargo carrier Enimex.

This shot provides an interesting comparison of the 'before and after' liveries worn by Enimex aircraft. The recently purchased An-72 on the right is still in basic Aeroflot colours.

15-2258	An-74	365.470.121.1053	2103
15-2259	An-74	365.470.121.1055	2104
15-2260	An-74	365.470.121.1058	2105
15-2261	An-74	365.470.121.1059	2106

LATVIA

• In April 2001 **RAF-Avia**, originally the flying detachment of the Riga Automobile Factory (hence the RAF), took delivery of a single An-74TK-100 to augment its fleet of An-26 freighters. (The factory is long since bankrupt and gone, but the airline lives on.) The aircraft – ex-Aviacor RA-74025, c/n 365.470.95.905, f/n 1407 – was duly reregistered YL-RAF in continuation of RAF-Avia's customised series and received the airline's stylish livery. It is believed that YL-RAF was briefly leased to the Ukrainian airline CABI as UR-CAE.

• The fleet of start-up airline **K.S. Avia** comprises two An-74s – Khar'kov-built YL-KSA (ex-RA-74030, c/n 365.470.98.957, f/n 1709) and Omsk-built YL-KSB (ex-UR-CAC, c/n 47136013, f/n 1809/0103P).

LAOS

In October 1998 the **Laotian government flight** took delivery of a single An-74TK-100 registered RDPL-3.4018 (c/n 365.470.99.1005, f/n 2001). It may be configured as a 52-seater, a freighter or a combi aircraft.

LIBYA

• **Libyan Arab Air Cargo [–/LCR]**, a commercial division of the **Libyan Arab Republic Air Force** (LARAF, or *al Quwwat al-Jawwiya al-Libiya*), operated at least one An-72 (presumably ex-Russian Air Force RA-72929, c/n 365.720.60.653, f/n 0610). Oddly, the aircraft was registered not in Libya but in Equatorial Guinea as 3C-QTA; still, the basic livery of Libyan Arab Air Cargo and the Libyan flag aft of the flightdeck spoke for themselves.

• A new multi-national airline named **Sin-Sad** (or **Sin-Saïd**) was set up in 2000 as an affiliate of Centrafricain Airlines with bases at Ras al Khaimah (UAE) and Tripoli (Libya). It is associated with the CEN-SAD organisation (Community of Sahel-Saharan States), and its aircraft are registered in Libya and Liberia. The Liberian ones included An-72 EL-ALL (ex-Enimex ES-NOL, c/n 365.720.80.789, f/n 0809) registered in August 2000.

However, just a year later new management entered office at the Liberian Civil Aviation Authority and the new broom started sweeping clean at once, cancelling the registration in May 2001. Hence EL-ALL moved to the Equatorial Guinean register, serving with West Africa Air as 3C-QQS.

• The **Libyan government** has ordered two An-74TK-200Ss, the as-yet non-existent ambulance version.

PERU

• In September 1992 **Aero Tumi**, an airline based at Lima-Jorge Chavéz International airport, took delivery of three An-72Vs – in theory at least (see below). They were registered OB-1485 (c/n 365.470.95.907, f/n 1408), OB-1486 (c/n 365.720.96.911, f/n 1501) and OB-1487 (c/n 365.720.96.912, f/n 1502) and were probably ex-CCCP-72978, CCCP-72981 and CCCP-72983 respectively.

The third aircraft is something of a mystery. Firstly, the Peruvian civil aircraft register quoted OB-1487 for a Cessna 172TK; secondly, an An-72 registered RA-72983 but wearing full Aero Tumi colours was seen at Zhukovskiy in September 1993. Quite possibly this aircraft was never exported after all.

• According to press reports, by May 1994 all three An-72Vs had been transferred to the **Peruvian Air Force** (FAP – *Fuerza Aérea del Peru*), retaining their civil registrations. At least one aircraft, OB-1486, also wore a military serial (398); it was placed in storage in 1996.

• After being withdrawn from military service OB-1485 found further use with **Colibri Airlines**. It was grounded again in 2001 and sold to São Tomé & Principe that year, becoming S9-BOU.

RWANDA

Evidence exists of a Rwandan-registered An-72, 9XR-CV (c/n unknown), operated by **Regional International Air Services** in 2003. Later, an anonymous-looking An-72 registered 9XR-RV (c/n unknown) was logged in May 2004. Interestingly, the aircraft was operating for the Libyan Arab Republic Air Force.

SÃO TOMÉ & PRINCIPE

As noted above, in 2001 an unidentified airline in São Tomé & Principe bought An-72V OB-1485, which gained the new registration S9-BOU. Another example registered S9-GRE and bearing no titles or logo was around in 1999-2000.

SINGAPORE

Air Mark Aviation based at Singapore-Seletar wet-leased An-74T-200 UR-74026 from Motor-Sich in 1996.

SOUTH AFRICAN REPUBLIC

The cargo carrier **Romoco Cargo S. A.** leased An-74 UR-74026 from Motor-Sich between November 1995 and February 1996. The 'S. A.' stood for 'South Africa'. Curiously, the aircraft carried the international civil security symbol (similar to that on EMERCOM or French *Securité Civile* aircraft) on the fin.

SWAZILAND

Air Pass, alias **Air Cess (Swaziland), Ltd.**, operated two former Russian Air Force An-72s bought in 1998: 3D-RTV (ex-RA-72934, c/n 365.720.80.777, f/n 0802) and 3D-RTW (ex-RA-72944, c/n 365.720.90.796, f/n 0902). 'Pass' was an acronym for Pietersburg Aviation Services & Systems; this was because, though nominally a Swazi company, the airline was based at Pietersburg-Gateway International airport, South Africa. In 1998 Air Pass suspended operations, selling almost its entire fleet to Centrafricain Airlines; thus 3D-RTV and 3D-RTW became TL-ACV and TL-ACW respectively.

UK

Atlantic Airlines [–/AAG] operate An-72 ES-NOI leased from Enimex in May 2004. Additionally, An-74 UR-74057 (c/n 365.470.98.960, f/n 1801) was leased from CABI Airlines on 13th January 2003 for a two-year term.

Above: A Mercedes-Benz G series jeep is driven into the freight hold of An-74 HK-3809-X of Helitaxi Colombia (ex-CCCP-74007, c/n 365.470.95.903, f/n 1406). Note the Colombian flag at the base of the fin.

Above: Seen here staging through Malta-Luqa airport, An-72 3C-QTA (ex-RA-72929, c/n 365.720.60.653, f/n 0610) wears the basic colours of Libyan Air Cargo.

An-74-200 UR-74026 (c/n 365.470.96.919, f/n 1506) is pictured here at Johannesburg-International in December 1995. Note the international civil security symbol on the tail.

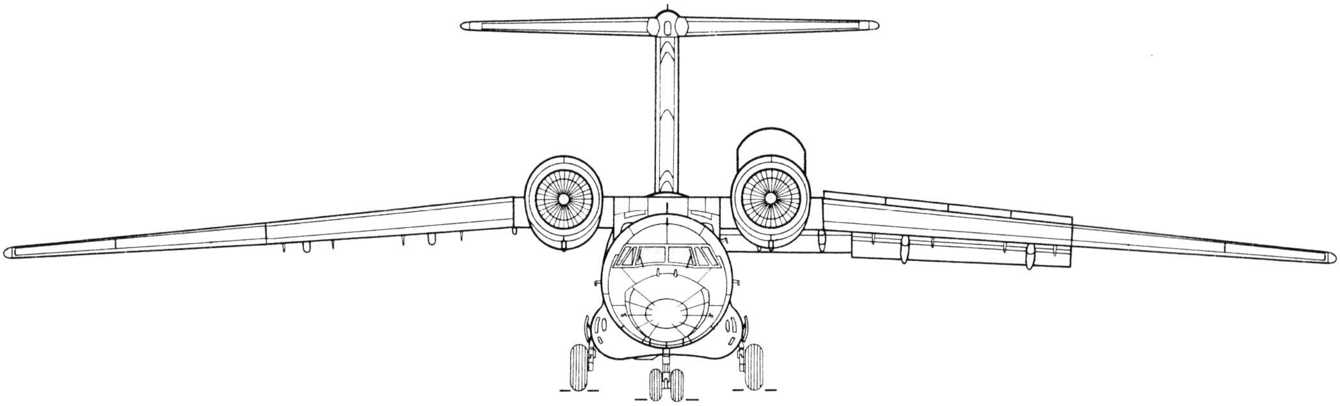

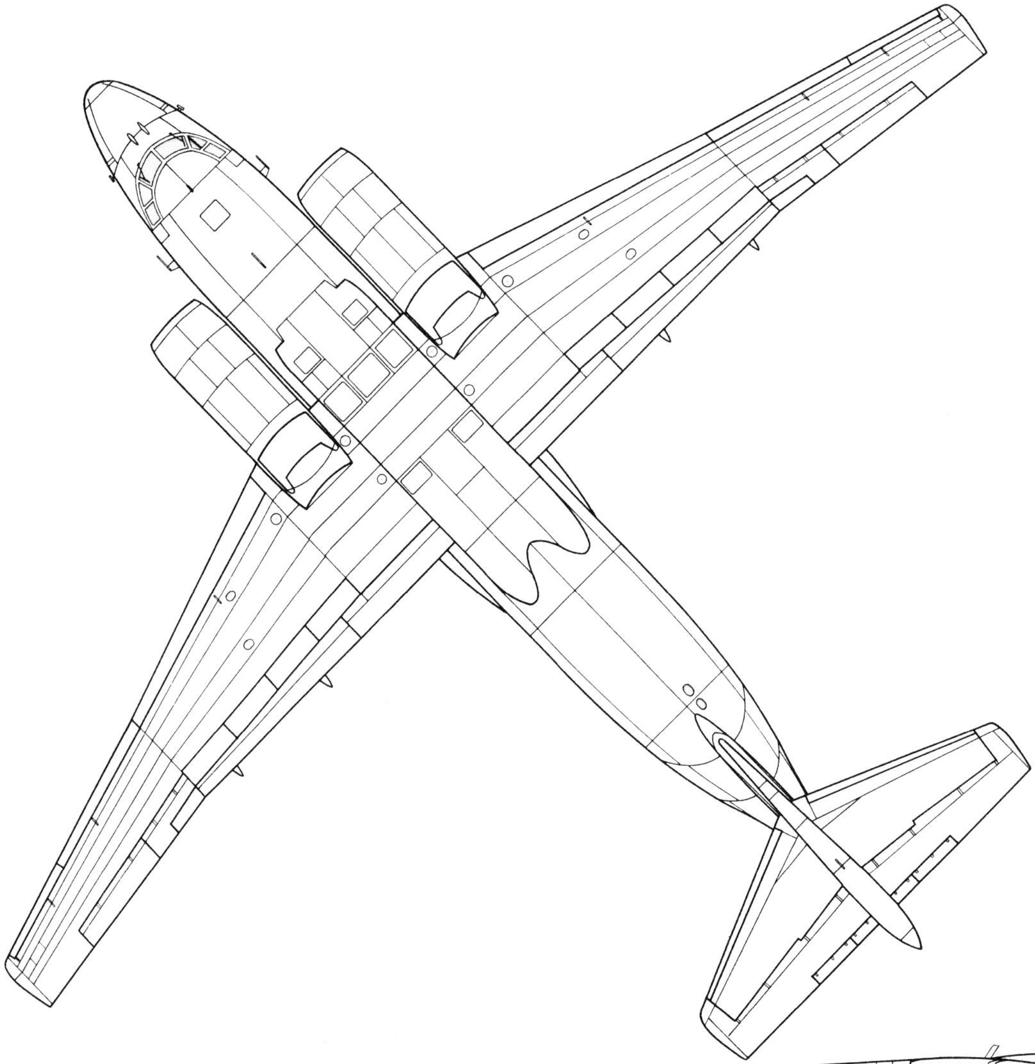

A three-view of the production-standard An-72.

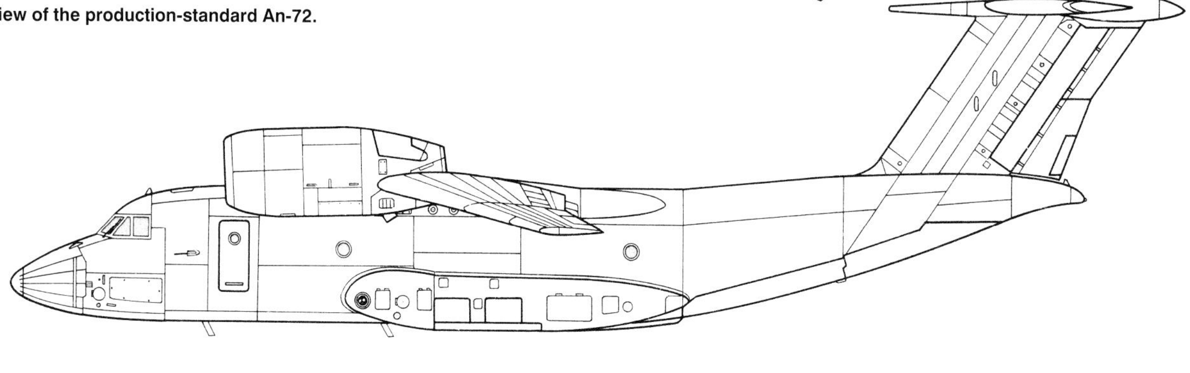

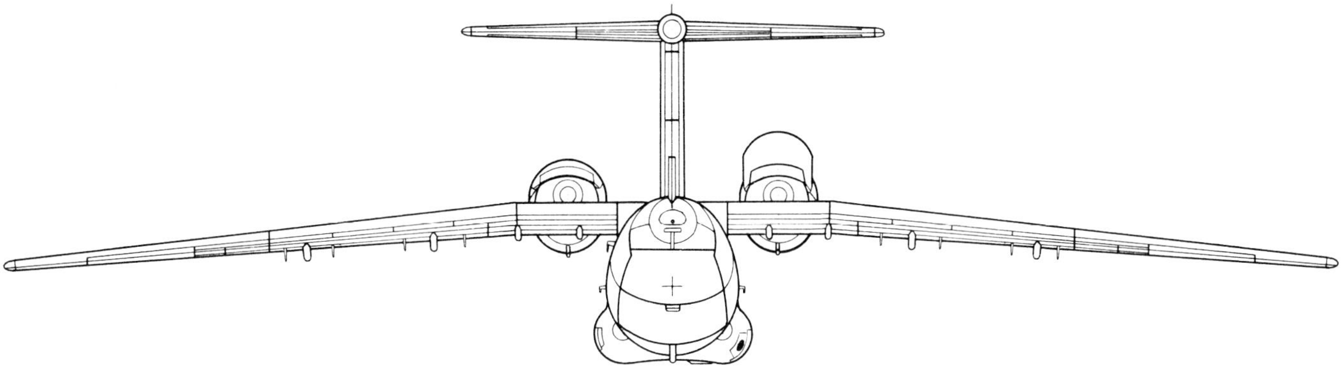

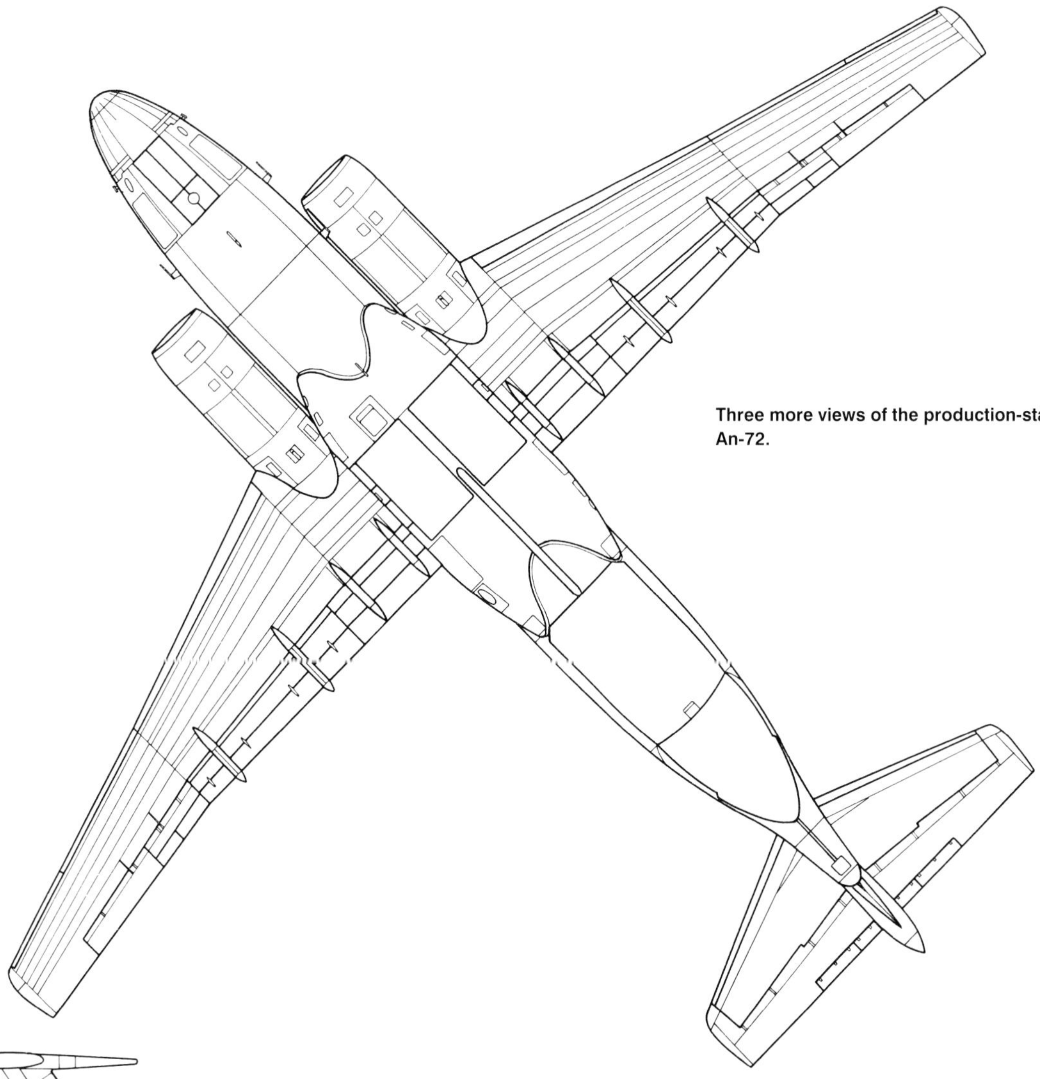

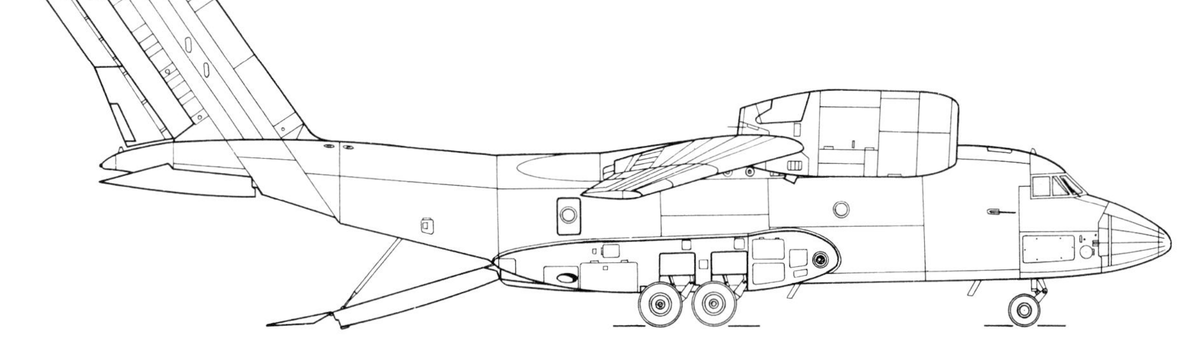

Three more views of the production-standard An-72.

The first and second prototypes of the An-72 as originally flown.

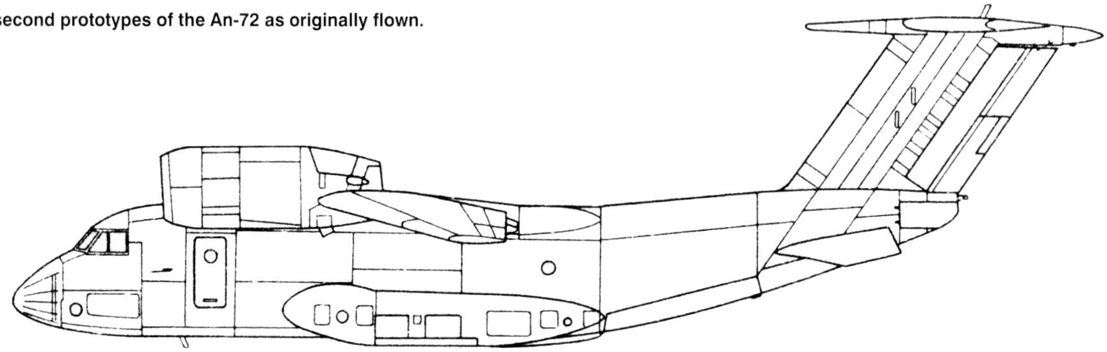

The first and second prototypes of the An-72 following modifications.

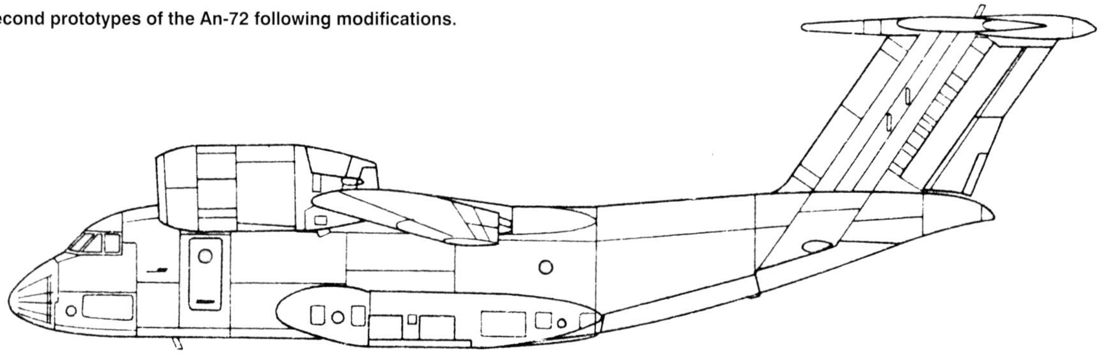

The production An-72 following modifications.

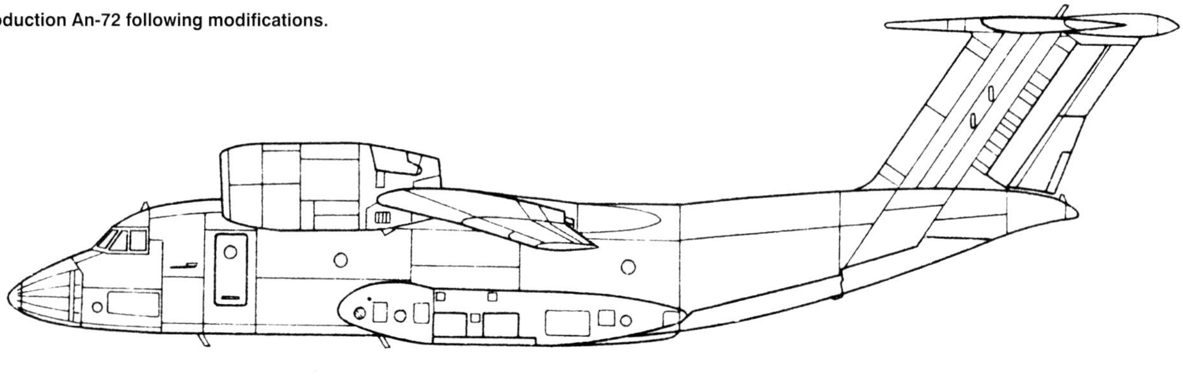

The prototype of the An-72P (c/n 006).

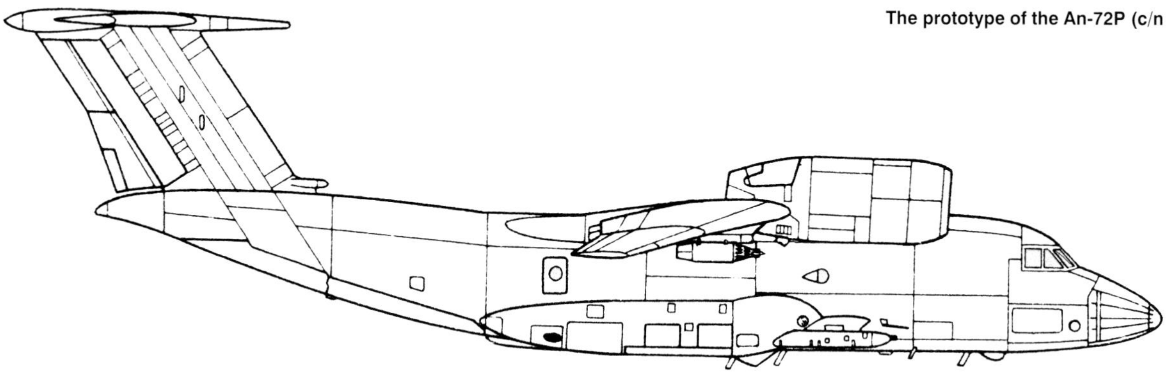

The An-72A (An-74) prototype as originally flown (CCCP-780334).

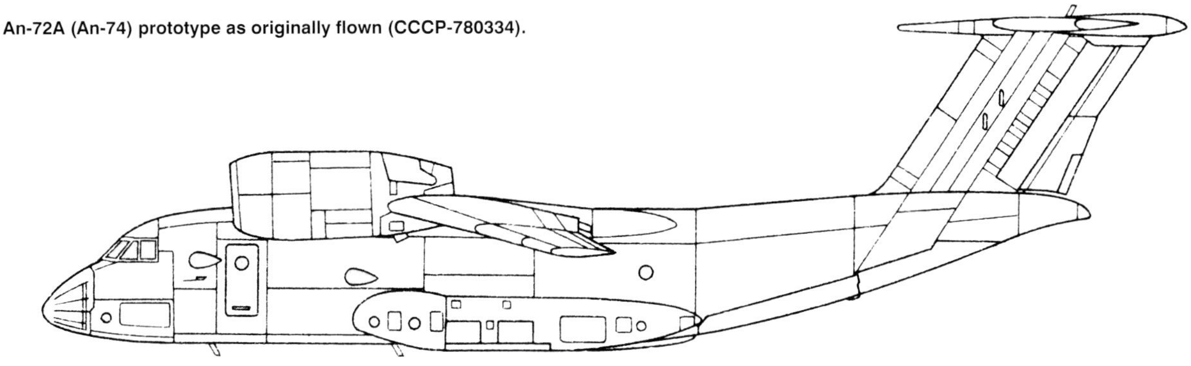

The same aircraft following modifications (CCCP-72003/CCCP-72200).

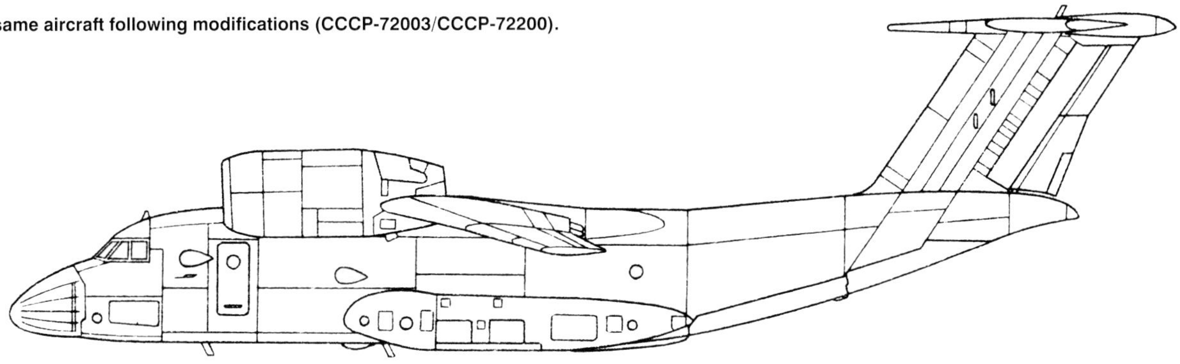

The pre-production An-74 (CCCP-58642).

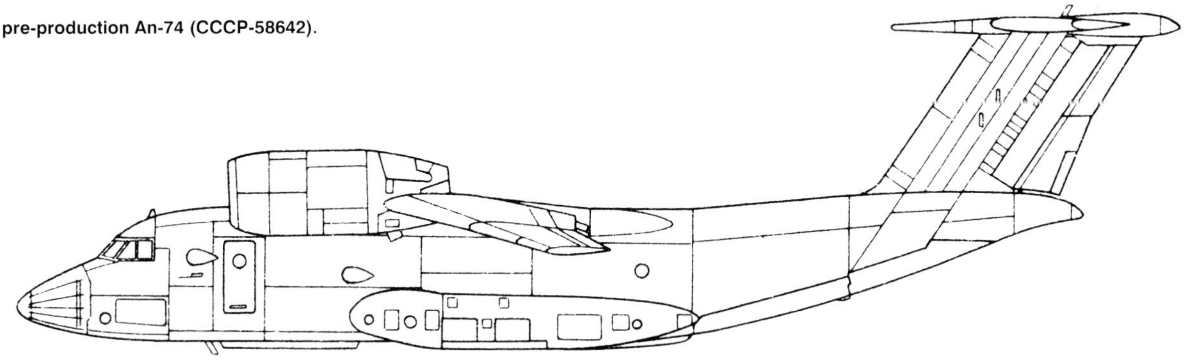

A typical production An-74.

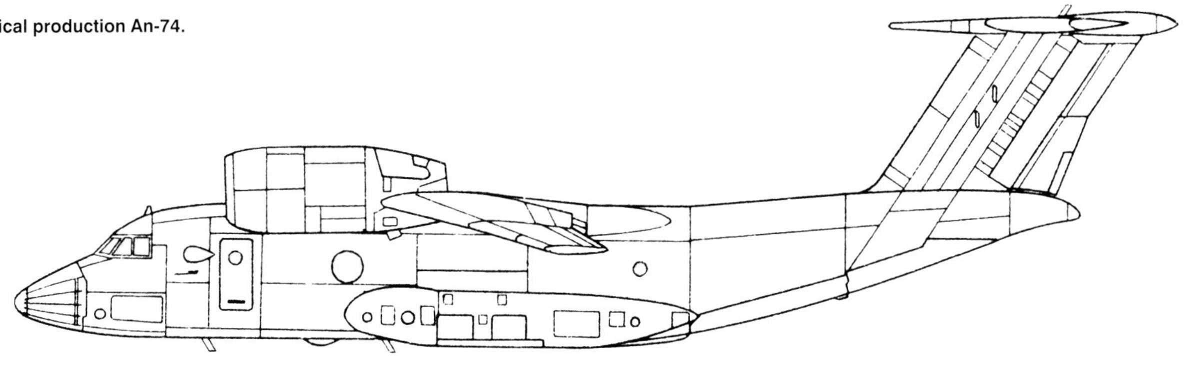

We hope you enjoyed this book . . .

Midland Publishing titles are edited and designed by an experienced and enthusiastic team of specialists.

We always welcome ideas from authors or readers for books they would like to see published.

In addition, our associate, Midland Counties Publications, offers an exceptionally wide range of aviation, military, naval and transport books and videos for sale by mail-order worldwide.

For a copy of the appropriate catalogue, or to order further copies of this book, and any other Midland Publishing titles, please write, telephone, fax or e-mail to:

Midland Counties Publications
4 Watling Drive, Hinckley,
Leics, LE10 3EY, England
Tel: (+44) 01455 254 450
Fax: (+44) 01455 233 737
E-mail: midlandbooks@compuserve.com
www.midlandcountiessuperstore.com

US distribution by Specialty Press – see page 2.

Earlier titles in the series:

Vols 1 to 4 are still available
Vol.5: Yakovlev's Piston-Engined Fighters
Vol.6: Polikarpov's Biplane Fighters
Vol.7: Tupolev Tu-4 Soviet Superfortress
Vol.8: Russia's Ekranoplans
Vol.9: Tupolev Tu-160 *Blackjack*
Vol.10: Lavochkin's Piston-Engined Fighters
Vol.11: Myasishchev M-4 & 3M
Vol.12: Antonov's Turboprop Twins
Vol.13: Mikoyan's Piston-Engined Fighters

Red Star Volume 14
MIL Mi-8/Mi-17
Rotary-Wing Workhorse and Warhorse

Yefim Gordon and Dmitriy Komissarov

Since 1961, when it first took to the air, the basic design of the Mi-8 has evolved. Every known version, both civil and military, is covered, including electronic warfare, minelaying and minesweeping and SAR. It also served as a basis for the Mi-14 amphibious ASW helicopter.
Over the years the Mi-8 family have become veritable aerial workhorses, participating in countless wars of varying scale. The type is probably best known for its service in the Afghan War.

Softback, 280 x 215 mm, 128 pages
179 b/w and 32 colour photographs, plus line drawings.
1 85780 161 X **£18.99**

Red Star Volume 15
ANTONOV AN-2
Annushka, Maid of All Work

Yefim Gordon and Dmitriy Komissarov

Initially derided as 'obsolete at the moment of birth' due to its biplane layout, this aircraft has put the sceptics to shame. It may lack the glamour of the fast jets, but it has proved itself time and time again as an indispensable and long-serving workhorse. The An-2, which first flew in 1947, has been operated by more than 40 nations.
The An-2 is the only biplane transport which remained in service long enough to pass into the 21st century!

Softback, 280 x 215 mm, 128 pages
c200 b/w and 28 colour photographs, plus line drawings.
1 85780 162 8 **£18.99**

Red Star Volume 16
SUKHOI INTERCEPTORS
The Su-9/-11/-15 and other types

Yefim Gordon

From 1953 Sukhoi produced a line of delta-winged interceptors including the Su-9 in 1958 followed in 1959 by the T-47/Su-11. A new line was started in 1960 with the twinjet T-58 which entered production as the Su-15. This aircraft remained a key element of the Soviet Air Defence Force well into the 1980s. Various versions of the Su-15 are detailed, as are the experimental PT-7/PT-8, T-49 and the unusual two-seat P-1 heavy interceptor.

Softback, 280 x 215 mm, 128 pages
189 b/w photos,14pp of colour, plus line drawings.
1 85780 180 6 **£18.99**

Red Star Volume 17
EARLY SOVIET JET BOMBERS
The 1940s and Early 1950s

Yefim Gordon

The Soviet Union put German technology to good use when developing its own jet bombers. The first to fly in the USSR was the Junkers EF131. This was followed by the EF140 and the equally unusual T-tailed, Baade 'aircraft 150'. The first wholly indigenous jet bomber was the four-engined IL-22 of 1947. Other experimental Ilyushins – the IL-30, IL-46 and IL-54 are described, as are the Tupolev 'aircraft 77', 'aircraft 82' and the 'aircraft 72/73/78' series.

Softback, 280 x 215 mm, 128 pages
116 b/w photos, 57 b/w illustrations, 14pp of line drawings.
1 85780 181 4 **£18.99**

Red Star Volume 18
ANTONOV'S HEAVY TRANSPORTS

Y Gordon, D and S Komissarov

In recent times the Antonov design bureau has created a number of heavy transport types. In this volume the An-22 four turboprop aircraft is examined in detail as is the An-124, the Soviet answer to the C-5 Galaxy. Originally designed as a military freighter the An-124 has also found a niche in the civil market, as has its outsize six-engined development the An-225. The book is completed by a history and description of the propfan driven An-70 tactical transport, which is under development.

Softback, 280 x 215 mm, 128 pages
189 b/w photos, 15pp of colour
1 85780 182 2 **£18.99**

Red Star Volume 19
SOVIET HEAVY INTERCEPTORS

Yefim Gordon

In the nervous 1950s, the Soviet Union faced the task of defending its borders against intrusions by Western spyplanes or bomber attacks. Aircraft developed for this priority long-range interception task included Mikoyan's I-3, I-7U, I-75 and Ye-152 which paved the way for the MiG-25, Sukhoi's T-37, terminated before it had a chance to fly, and Tupolev's Tu-128 – so huge it was mistaken for a medium bomber in the West.

Softback, 280 x 215 mm, 128 pages
159 b/w photos, 12pp of colour, plus 23pp of line drawings
1 85780 191 1 **£18.99**

Red Star Volume 20
SOVIET/RUSSIAN UNMANNED AERIAL VEHICLES

Yefim Gordon

The Lavochkin OKB's La-17, produced in target drone and recce versions, was the first Soviet UAV to find large-scale use. The Tupolev OKB also developed a line of UAVs, including the Tu-123 Yastreb, Tu-141 Strizh, Tu-243 Reys and the latest Tu-300 recce/strike UAV. Yakovlev's unmanned aircraft are also covered including the Pchela (Bee) surveillance UAV. Mention is also made of UAVs and drones developed by such companies as Strela and the Moscow Aviation Institute.

Softback, 280 x 215 mm, 128 pages
143 b/w photos, 29pp of colour, plus line drawings
1 85780 193 8 **£18.99**